Living that Matters

Living by God's Design

Sam Lewis

WESTBOW
PRESS®
A DIVISION OF THOMAS NELSON
& ZONDERVAN

Scripture quotations taken from the New American Standard Bible®,
Copyright © 1960, 1962, 1963, 1968, 1971, 1972, 1973, 1975, 1977, 1995
by The Lockman Foundation. Used by permission. (www.Lockman.org)

WestBow Press books may be ordered through booksellers or by contacting:

WestBow Press
A Division of Thomas Nelson & Zondervan
1663 Liberty Drive
Bloomington, IN 47403
www.westbowpress.com
1 (866) 928-1240

ISBN: 978-1-5127-0969-8 (sc)
ISBN: 978-1-5127-0968-1 (hc)
ISBN: 978-1-5127-0967-4 (e)

Library of Congress Control Number: 2015913620

Print information available on the last page.

WestBow Press rev. date: 08/27/2015

Contents

Preface

I have spent over forty years listening to, observing, and coaching people in relationships. I have learned a great deal from those years of experience about how people relate. Those experiences have given me many illustrations and some understanding that will help me to articulate the principles and values that I want to share with you in this book.

However, I did not learn these principles and values from that experience. I learned them through careful study of God's Word while asking Him for wisdom to understand how He designed His universe. That study was guided by some amazing mentors, men of God who invested in my life.

Often- during the many years I have been teaching these principles, people have asked me why I have not written a book on the things that I teach. My answer was twofold. First, I said it was because the book has already been written. It is called the Bible. But the real reason was because, while books can give you information, inspiration, or even an inclination toward right living, they rarely ensure transformation.

In my experience, transformation is better attained through accountability and constant, consistent reaffirmation of truth. I call this *coaching*. The Bible calls it *discipleship*. If you want to get the most out of this book as a couple, then find a mature, godly couple to read it with you and hold you accountable for what you learn here.

Every athlete and every team, no matter how good they are, need coaches. There have been teams composed of the greatest athletes in the world who failed because of poor coaching. There have been teams with mediocre athletes who succeeded with great coaching.

I believe reading this book can help your marriage grow. But if you want to revolutionize your marriage as well as your entire life, then get a mentor, which is just another word for coach. It is with this hope in mind that I write this book.

One final note before you continue reading. This book is really not meant simply to be read; it is intended to be studied. It is a manual to help you live by God's design and then pass it on. If you find that you agree with these values, then use this book to teach others, but especially your children and grandchildren. I will show you in the book and linked resources how to do that. Please read the entire introduction and watch the linked video at the end before deciding you know what this book is about.

Introduction

All relationships encounter conflict. This is not always a bad thing. Some conflict is healthy. It helps us to grow. The Bible says, ***"As iron sharpens iron, so one man sharpens another."(Proverbs 27:17)*** This kind of conflict is usually a result of the fact that we have different personalities and different perceptions of what we see. Two people can be looking the same thing and see two completely different things. This is why the Bible teaches us that facts should be confirmed by two or three witnesses.

If you look at something while covering one eye at a time, switching back and forth, you will notice that the image shifts just slightly when viewed from each eye. When both eyes are open, we have a stereoscopic view that is the most accurate view. When our brain connects the two images as one, it gives us things like depth perception and color enhancement. If we learn to trust that together we have a better view than we do alone, then our differences can help us to grow.

Resolving this type of conflict has to do with learning to communicate. It is learning that not only do men/"Martians" and women/"Venusians" speak different languages, but every family has its own language. I have met couples who have been married for many years and are still speaking to each other in foreign languages.

I am not speaking about learning the "Five Love Languages." Learning tools like that can be helpful, but God has given us a very well-articulated language of love that transcends male, female, and every other human language.

A major hindrance that turns healthy conflict into unhealthy conflict is our personal issues. By personal issues, I mean wrong programming and wrong ways of thinking. This wrong programming creates filters that cause us to misinterpret the actions and words of our spouses. It often causes us to react in hurt or anger instead of being able to grow from conflict. I believe that this wrong programming leads to what the Bible calls *strongholds* or *fortresses*.

For though we walk in the flesh, we do not war according to the flesh, for the weapons of our warfare are not of the flesh, but divinely powerful for the destruction of fortresses.(strongholds) We are destroying speculations and every lofty thing raised up against the knowledge of God, and we are taking every thought captive to the obedience of God. (2 Corinthians10:3–5 NASB)

I have much more to say about dealing with personal issues and healthy conflict, but that is for another book another time. However, it will be profitable to give you at least some principles that are vital to experiencing healthy conflict and that will also help you to apply what you learn in this book. These principles can temporarily counterbalance our personal issues, but those issues still need to be dealt with.

First, let me give you my modified definition of *principles* for the purpose of understanding this book. Principles are ways of understanding how to bridge the gap from values or beliefs to right behavior. In a sense I would call principles *applied wisdom.* Let me give you two principles to help foster healthy conflict. Later you will see how right values make this possible.

1) *I must learn to respond to actions rather than react to motives.* Much of the hurt and resulting anger that happen in relationships come about when we assess another's motive. In other words, it is not just the action that hurts but the motive behind the action. A spouse may speak in a certain way, and you may think something like "She is just trying to get back at me for yesterday" or "He is just doing that because he is jealous." Often, actions or words in and of themselves are benign. They do not become hurtful until we add motive. The biggest problem with motive is that you cannot prove or disprove motive.

If my wife has asked me to do something and I have forgotten to do it, she may think the reason (my motive) is that I do not care about her. I have no way to prove to her that is not the reason, any more than she could prove that it is. If she reacts to that motive, it will be very hurtful for her, and she may become angry. If she says something to me about it in anger, I may think that the reason (her motive) is because she wants to control everything I do and she does not appreciate what I do for her. This will escalate and cause a lot of pain. Before long the original offense (action) is completely forgotten.

I am not saying that motive has no importance at all. You might be right about the motive. But reacting to motive seldom has a good result. Much of the time we do not understand why we ourselves do what we do, much less why others do what they do. The truth is that there can be many reasons or motives behind an action. What I am saying is that in wisdom, we will do better to *respond* to the action on its own merits rather than *react* to motive. The only way to accomplish this is by learning the second principle.

2) ***I must learn to live and act according to what I know rather than what I feel.*** What I feel is neither good nor bad; it just is. I simply cannot trust what I feel. My feelings do not know or care about the difference between truth and fantasy. If I am sitting in a theater, watching a scary movie, I know it is not real. I know it is just actors. However, my heart may be beating fast, my palms sweating, and my breathing becoming rapid. My emotions do not care that it is just a movie.

I do not always have control over what I feel, but I do always have control over what I do. Notice two words that I used earlier in speaking about the principle of motive: *react* versus *respond*. We generally react (and usually overreact) to what we feel, but we respond to what we know. If I am sitting in that theater and I react to what I feel, I may run out of the theater in fear. If I respond to what I know, I will choose knowledge over my feelings and tough it out. Likewise, in regard to motive, I want to respond to the action rather than react to the motive.

I React According to What I Feel; I Respond According to What I Know

The only person who can make this choice is you. Only you can choose not to assess motive. Only you can decide to respond rather than react. So here is a helpful hint. If someone says or does something to you that could be taken in more than one way, one of those being good and the other is bad ... *choose the good way!*

Unhealthy Conflict

Not all conflict is healthy. Some conflict not only does not help us to grow, it actually hinders our growth. This kind of conflict usually comes from the fact that, more often than not, we have different *values*. In order for us to completely understand why this is important, I need to define what I mean by values. I will do this in a moment, but first I must let you know why this kind of conflict is so dangerous.

There has been a great deal written about conflict resolution. There are many strategies that are taught by the world and by Christian teachers. Some of it is good in certain situations but flawed when it comes to resolving the conflict caused by having different values. Most of these strategies can be summed up in the following five styles developed by Kenneth Thomas and Ralph Kilmann in the 1970s:

- Accommodate (I Lose, You Win)
- Avoid (I Lose, You Lose)
- Compromise (We Both Lose, We Both Win)
- Compete (I Win, You Lose)
- Collaborate (I Win, You Win)

Many relationship "experts" say that the best of these is to collaborate, since it has win-win. But in reality, even collaboration comes down to compromise.

The problem with all of these methods is that each of them, even if successful on the surface, has the same damaging effect. What really happens with all of these is that one or perhaps both parties must violate their values. One yields values to the other, usually whoever is most dominant in that area. It is very hurtful to violate your own values even if they are the wrong values. This often leads to bitterness and anger. The real solution is for both of you to have the same values. One purpose of this book is to show you how you can both have the same value system without compromise.

Now let me share with you my definition of values for the purpose of this book. If you look online, you will discover many definitions of values or value systems. My favorite is from Wikipedia. It says "Value (personal and cultural) the principles, standards, or quality which guides human actions." Most people think they know what their values are, but our values are not shown by what we say we believe. They're shown by how we behave. Our values determine our behavior, and it could also be said that our behavior reveals our values.

I want to take this a step further. God designed the universe and everything in it to work in a certain way. It works that way every single time. It never changes. When we follow that design, life works, and when we violate that design, life doesn't work.

I believe that God's Word and God's law as written in the Bible are His human articulation of how He designed the universe to work.

Because His universe always works as He designed it, and because His laws are simply His articulation of that design, it is therefore impossible to break God's laws. It is we who will be broken.

If you jump off of a ten-story building, you will not break the law of gravity. You will break your neck. It does not matter if you believe in the law of gravity or understand the law of gravity or agree with the law of gravity. You will still break your neck.

The same is true in the positive. We do not have to understand or agree with the laws of aerodynamics to get in an airplane and go up in the sky. All of God's laws, i.e., His design, work the same way whether we understand them or not, whether we believe them or not.

If God's law or God's design does not depend on my belief, then what is the importance of belief? While my belief does not change the design, it does affect the way that I interact with it. For example, if I am on top of that ten-story building and I do not believe in gravity, I will behave very differently than I would if I did believe.

Every difficulty that we face in life, whether personal or relational, can be traced back to a violation of God's design. His design for relationship is perfect, and when we relate according to His design, it always works. When we struggle with relationships, we want to blame everything in the world except the possibility that maybe somewhere God's design is being violated.

Adam and Eve violated God's design for relationships. (I will explain how in chapter 3.) When they did, it left Eve vulnerable to Satan's temptation to eat the fruit of the knowledge of good and evil. It was not God's design for us to have that knowledge. The Bible says we should be *"excellent at what is right and innocent of evil."* Much of counseling focuses on trying to fix what is wrong. We should be focused on learning what is right. This book is not designed to help you fix your problems. It is designed to teach you how to live according to God's design. When you do, it will erase the source of those problems. God's design is perfect. When things go wrong, it is not a faulty design; rather, it is operator error.

I remember when I bought my first brand-new car, it came with a warranty. (It was a 1974 Camaro, in case you were wondering.) The manufacturer guaranteed that my car would go 50,000 miles without any breakdown of the engine and drivetrain.

The warranty, however, was conditional. The manufacturer tested the car and determined that indeed the car would travel 50,000 miles *if* certain things were followed. I had to change the oil every 6,000 miles, get a tune-up every 12,000 miles, and check and maintain fluid levels.

Therein lay the difficulty: I rarely changed or even checked my oil, I seldom got a tune-up, and I never, ever checked my fluids.

At around 30,000 miles, I began to have engine trouble. I decided I had bought a lemon and determined that I would never buy this brand of car again. I blamed the manufacturer. In reality, the engine trouble was due to operator error.

God designed life to work a certain way. Because He designed it, He knows how it must be lived in order to give us the peace and joy we all desire. There are conditions to his "warranty." They are made very clear in His owner's manual: the Bible.

The Bible is full of phrases that contain "if" and "then." *If* you do this, *then* that will happen. But we live life our own way, often ignoring His clear design. Then when things go wrong and life doesn't seem to work right, we blame the manufacturer, our Creator. Again I say, in reality, it is operator error.

The Owner's Manual

It is important that we are in agreement as to how we know what God's design is. I stated earlier that I believe that God's laws, i.e., His Word, are His human articulation of how He designed the universe. Therefore, if we are to be unified in our values (the way we view His design), we must agree on some basic facts about the Bible.

Some may take issue with my statement that His laws are His human articulation of His design. Let me give you an example so we are clear on what I mean by that. In the Old Testament, thousands of years ago, God gave very strict laws about what to do if you came in contact with something unclean, such as a sick person, a dead person, or an unclean animal. These laws described a detailed ceremony you had to perform to become clean again.

We are no longer under obligation to that ceremonial law, but the design behind the law is still true. Do you realize that we did not discover germs until about two hundred years ago? God's law teaches us His design.

I believe that the Bible was inspired by God and is literally true. There is much debate about what it means to be "inspired by God." I don't remember where I got this definition, but I am in full agreement with it: "God the Holy Spirit so supernaturally directed the human writers of Scripture that, without waiving their intelligence, their individuality, their personal feelings, their literary style, or any other human factor of expression, His complete and coherent message to mankind was recorded with perfect accuracy in the original languages of Scripture: the very words bearing the Authority of Divine Authorship."

I believe that includes every word and even spelling. (of the original Greek and Hebrew) I also believe that the Bible means exactly the same today as it did the day it was written. We may grow in our understanding. We may differ on some fine points of application. But the meaning never changes. His design does not change or evolve. What was true for one generation is true for all generations.

This is very important to understanding God's design. There are many who believe that certain things in Scripture were true for the culture and time it was written but have different meaning in our culture today. While I do believe that understanding the culture in which the Bible was written is vital to accurately understanding its meaning, that meaning does not change with changing culture.

I put a great deal of Scripture in this book to show the source of these values, but I need to make it clear that this is not a book on theology. I do not have room here for a detailed study of every verse. However, it must be understood that the Bible is the source and authority for understanding God's design. The Bible overrules science, culture, psychology, or anecdotal stories that may be in opposition.

It is because I believe this so strongly that I have not simply used Scripture references for you to look up, as many books do. I believe that very few people take the time to actually look those verses up and read them. I cannot take that chance. In most cases, I have printed the entire passage here so that you can see where these values come from.

The Bible may not tell us everything that we want to know, but it does tell us everything we need to know and everything that God intends for us to know.

"The secret things belong to the Lord our God, but the things revealed belong to us and to our sons forever, that we may observe all the words of this law." (Deuteronomy 29:29 NASB)

If it is meant for us to know, it is in the Bible.

This book is not meant to be exhaustive, meaning I cannot include everything about God's design. I hope it will be a template for you to spend a lifetime on the journey to the discovery of just how awesome His design is. Chapter 1 explains how this template will work.

Once you have read the book and followed the many links to outside resources (videos, articles, etc.), I invite you to visit our Web site, www.livingthatmatters.com/. There, you will find more resources to help you live these values and pass them on generationally.

Please watch this video before reading further so I can explain my vision of where I hope this book will lead you.

Living That Matters Vision
www.livingthatmattersbook.com/01.html

For help with personal issues that come from spiritual issues, I highly recommend this series.

50 days of transformation
www.livingthatmattersbook.com/02.html

Note: All of the links/QR codes in this book can be found at www.livingthatmatters.com. Under the resource tab, click on links from the book and you will find all of the videos, articles and webpages on one page.

Perhaps everything in your life until now has just been the introduction. Let us partner with you in writing Chapter 1 of the story of your family. It is a story that can be written backward and forward as you discover God's true design and purpose for your life.

www.livingthatmatters.com
Introduction complete...

CHAPTER 1

My Value System

I now come back to *values*. For the purpose of this book, I define values as how we perceive the way God designed the universe. For example, if we perceive God's design in marriage is that a man is supposed to be the "boss" of his wife, then that is our value about the marriage relationship. That value will determine our behavior.

This is how we achieve a unified value system: by learning and understanding God's design. For most of us, the formation of a value system began with our parents. It was then influenced by things such as school and television and even our friends. Very few of us actually sat down and thought out and chose our values. They just developed. As I stated earlier, most of us don't even really know what our values are.

I want to bring you and your spouse to a unified value system. This is a lifelong process. In this book, I want to give you a template for that process by taking you through five value categories:

Spiritual Values
Relational Values
Parental Values
Sexual Values
Financial Values

I will share with you what I believe are God's top values/ designs in each of these categories. Remember that a value is how we perceive God's design. I will only be discussing mechanics and practical application of these values insofar as it helps me to illustrate the value. Right behavior comes from right thinking. In this book I am only asking you to adopt these values as truth. It is being before doing.

Think of it like this. Your value system is like an operating system on your computer, such as Windows for PC or Snow Leopard for Mac. The operating system is there as a platform to run many other programs. Without it, other programs you put on your computer will not run properly. They may be great programs, but they need a proper platform to run on.

So much of counseling and teaching about marriage involves teaching "programs" such as good communication skills or parenting skills. These can be great, but if the relationship does not have the right operating system, they are destined to fail. This brings frustration. You feel like you are "following the program," and yet eventually you fall back into the same old behaviors.

Years ago a couple came to me as a last resort. They had been to see many counselors and, in their words, had faithfully followed all they were told. They had already filed for divorce, but on the recommendation of a friend decided to give me a try.

As they began to talk to me, I noticed that every argument led back to finances. They could not agree on anything when it came to money. In the course of different counseling attempts, they had tried compromising and communicating better to see the other's point of view. It had created such bitterness and mistrust that they could not even tell me the issues without spewing hateful attacks at each other.

I explained to them about their value systems and said I wanted to unify their financial values. First, I wanted to identify their top areas of financial dispute. It was like being in the middle of a war as we made a list of the top ten areas of conflict over finances. It took over an hour. I put that list away and spent the next few weeks teaching them God's financial values.

At the end of the teaching, I did with them what I will ask you to do at the end of each category. They compared their values to God's values. I asked them first to look at everything on their value list that was in direct opposition to God's values and to cross it off their list. Then I asked them to look for everything on their list that was in complete harmony with God's values and cross that off. You see, those were no longer their values but God's.

Then I took out the list of their top ten areas of financial disagreement. I read the first item and looked at the wife. I said, "According to God's values, what way should this be handled?" After she answered, I looked at her husband and asked, "Do you agree?"

He said, "Yes." I asked if he was sure, and he said he was.

I read the next item and asked him what the right thing to do was. Then I asked if she agreed with his answer, and she did.

I continued down the list in the same fashion, taking about five minutes to reach the end. I sat back in my chair and looked at them. I will never forget the look on the wife's face as she said, "It can't be that easy."

I asked them if they had both been honest and comfortable with their answers. They assured me they had. I said, "Then it is just that easy."

They withdrew their filing for divorce, and last time I talked with them, they were still doing well.

I am not saying it is always that simple. Sometimes there are many different issues involved. You will never be fully healthy in any of the five value categories until you are healthy in all of them. What I am saying is that you cannot work out the mechanics until you get the right operating system.

Reformatting Your Hard Drive

Recently I installed a new operating system on one of my computers. The install program asked me if I wanted to do a nondestructive install or a clean install. It "highly recommended" that I do a nondestructive install. Having a little computer experience, I understood why, but it made me laugh.

You see, to do a nondestructive install means that you install the new system over the top of the old one. Instead of replacing it, you simply upgrade it. All of your existing programs and data remain intact. The software makers recommend this because they do not want to be responsible for the loss of any of your data.

The reason I laughed is because no programmer worth his salt would recommend a nondestructive install over a clean install. The problem with a nondestructive install is that it not only preserves your programs and data but also any problems that may be there. There may be compatibility issues between old programs and the new operating system.

To do a clean install requires much more work and time. First you need to back up all of your data on a separate hard drive. Then, after you install the new system, you have to reinstall your old programs. Sometimes this can't be done. You might not have the original disks or even remember where you got the programs.

Yielding Your Rights to God

Making room for a new operating system

Philippians 2:1–7

In Philippians 2:2, Paul says, ***"Make my joy complete by being of the same mind, maintaining the same love, united in spirit, intent on one purpose."***

That is a description of a godly relationship. I believe that when two people are operating from the same value system, this is what their relationship will look like. This means that conflict over values is never healthy conflict.

Unfortunately there is one major obstacle standing in the way of you having that kind of unity with your spouse: you! That is why before we can even talk about getting the right values, you must first live and die by this one overarching value that guides all others. Part of it is the first line of chapter 1 in Rick Warren's book *The Purpose Driven Life*: *"IT'S NOT ABOUT YOU."* Because, as his book makes clear, *IT'S ABOUT GOD!* This is a phrase which I have used for many years and one that you will see throughout this book. *IT'S NOT ABOUT ME; IT'S ABOUT GOD!*

Notice the title of this section is not "Yielding Your Rights to Your Spouse." I stated in the introduction that it is very dangerous to violate your own value system even if that system is wrong. When we violate our value system, we create feelings of guilt and bitterness and anger. Many times in a sincere and often loving desire to compromise, we yield our rights to our mates. In so doing, we violate our values, and then those feelings of guilt, bitterness, and anger are directed toward our spouse.

When I talk about yielding your rights, I am talking about legitimate, God -given rights. It is not like saying, "I have a right to play golf seven days a week, but I will yield that right and only play once a week." I mean real rights. Do I have a right to be loved? Yes. Do I have a right to be treated with respect and dignity? Yes. I am asking you to yield *all* of your rights to God.

Do nothing from selfishness or empty conceit, but with humility of mind regard one another as more important than yourselves; do not merely look out for your own personal interest, but also for the interest of others. (Philippians 2:3– 4 NASB)

In effect this passage tells us to give up our own rights for the sake of others. I don't think he meant to yield them "to" others but rather "for" others. I am not asking you to compromise or to yield anything to your spouse. I am asking you to yield all of your rights to God.

The natural instinct here is to ask, "But if I yield all of my rights to God, then does that mean my spouse can treat me however he or she wants, and I just have to take it?" I will answer that in a moment, but if you are asking the question you are missing the point. Paul illustrates for us exactly what he means.

Have this attitude in yourselves which was also in Christ Jesus, who, although He existed in the form of God, did not regard equality with God a thing to be grasped, but emptied Himself, taking the form of a bond-servant, and being made in the likeness of men. Being found in appearance as a man, He humbled Himself by becoming obedient to the point of death, even death on a cross. (Philippians 2:5–8 NASB)

My friends, can you grasp the enormity of what he is saying? Imagine this. Imagine that you wake up one morning, and before you even open your eyes, you notice the foulest odor you ever smelled. Then you open your eyes and look around. You realize you are lying in the bottom of a sewer. There you see unmentionable, vile things floating all around you. The stench is overwhelming. But you also feel physically very strange.

You look up and notice a broken piece of mirror lying against the sewer wall. As you look in the mirror, you realize that you have woken up in the body of a big, disgusting sewer rat. Now imagine that you have done that willingly.

Jesus was in the glory and majesty of heaven, beautiful and pure. He was God. He was sovereign. He left all of that behind and limited Himself to human flesh in the midst of a sinful, fallen world. He was still God, but He yielded the right to function as God. This is why He said He could do nothing without His father (John 6:19, 30). In this human flesh, He was tortured and reviled and finally crucified. He did it all willingly. This was the most incredible act of yielding rights in all of history.

Now what was your question? Oh yes. "If I yield my rights, does this mean my spouse can treat me however he or she wants, and I just have to take it?" Sounds a little different now, doesn't it?

But I have good news for you. The answer is no. Once you yield all of your rights to God, you must now stand up for what is right because it *is* right, not because it is *your* right. As long as you are holding on to your rights and defending your rights, God cannot (will not) help you. And by the way, how is that working for you?

If you yield your rights to God, then, when those rights are violated, God is obligated to defend you. Trust me; He will do a better job of it than you. I understand that sometimes there can be a fine line between standing up for "my rights" and standing for "what is right." But I can tell you that my wife can tell the difference in me.

I hear couples saying things like "I am fed up with the way he treats me" or "I will not put up with her attitude anymore." These are clearly examples of people standing for their own rights.

I have a pastor friend who was once being accused of very hurtful things by men in his church. I was present in the meeting when they came to confront him. I knew that he was innocent of the charges, and I knew that he could prove it.

After the first man leveled his charges and stated how much the pastor's supposed actions hurt him, I waited for the pastor to defend himself and prove that he was not guilty. Instead my friend looked at the man and said, "That must have hurt you really bad. Will you forgive me?"

I was stunned. Why didn't he tell the man the truth?

The man began to weep and said to the pastor, "Yes, I forgive you. I love you and just couldn't believe you would say these things."

The pastor responded, "I cannot tell you how much it means to me that you believed I did this and yet were willing to forgive me. That is why I am so glad to be able to tell you that I did not do it, and I can prove it. It just means way more to me to have your unconditional love than to prove myself right."

This pastor had truly yielded his rights to God. It was not about being right; it was about *doing* the right thing.

Yielding your rights to God, truly believing that it is not about you, it is about God, is like reformatting your hard drive. It is the basis for letting go of your old value system. Even if you have all the "right" values, I ask you, "Are they your values or God's values?"

"Have this attitude in you which was also in Christ Jesus."

Now you can begin installing your operating system, better known as your value system.

www.livingthatmatters.com

Chapter 1 to be continued ...

CHAPTER 2

Spiritual Values

God's Design for Spirituality

Because all other values really come out of our spiritual values, there is much that can be said. I cannot possibly include it all in this book, but I will be referring you to some great resources.

All of the spiritual values I want to discuss center around three basic commitments. They are:

- Commitment to God (an intimate relationship)
- Commitment to the body of Christ (the church)
- Commitment to the world (unbelievers)

These three commitments are found in two passages of Scripture, sometimes called the Great Commandment and the Great Commission.

And he answered, "You shall love the Lord your God with all your heart, and with all your soul, and with all your strength, and with all your mind; and your neighbor as yourself." (Luke 10:27 NASB-U)

"Go therefore and make disciples of all the nations, baptizing them in the name of the Father and the Son and the Holy Spirit, teaching them to observe all that I commanded you; and lo, I am with you always, even to the end of the age." (Matthew 28:19–20 NASB)

Each commitment gives birth to the other. You cannot love God and not love His family. The commission to go and make disciples was given to the church, His body. If you are part of His body, you are part of the mission to take the good news to the world.

In his two books, *The Purpose Driven Church* and *The Purpose Driven Life*, Dr. Rick Warren does an excellent job fleshing out these values and how they apply to our lives, both individually and as a church. If you truly want to embrace the spiritual values, I recommend reading them.

Purpose Driven Life
www.livingthatmattersbook.com/03.html

Purpose Driven Church
www.livingthatmattersbook.com/04.html

Spiritual Value 1
We Are Designed for Intimate
Fellowship with God

Of course, the overarching value is also the number one *spiritual value*: it's not about me; it's about God. That God is sovereign is the foundation of the universe. That this sovereign God is knowable and that He wants to have intimate fellowship with me is the foundation of my life.

I want to remind you that my purpose in this book is not to teach you application as much as it is for these to truly become your values. This is especially true for this value. Let me explain what I mean.

I myself might have confidence even in the flesh. If anyone else has a mind to put confidence in the flesh, I far more: circumcised the eighth day, of the nation of Israel, of the tribe of Benjamin, a Hebrew of Hebrews; as to the Law, a Pharisee; as to zeal, a persecutor of the church; as to

***the righteousness which is in the Law, found blameless.
(Philippians 3:4–6 NASB-U)***

These words of Paul are what in his time would have been a description of a godly man. These were activities of faith that to his listeners put him far above the average religious man.

Let's translate this into our culture. I often hear statements such as "That guy is a really good Christian" or "I am not really a very good Christian." What do people mean when they say this? What is meant by "good Christian"?

These speakers may not be consciously aware of it, but I believe they are really referring to what I call the Big Five of Christianity. The Big Five are prayer, Bible study, church attendance, giving, and witnessing. We believe that the person who does these things well is a good Christian. You are a better or lesser Christian depending on how you measure up to this checklist. Usually when we feel like we aren't right with God, it is because we do not score well on the Big Five. But listen to what Paul goes on to say in his letter to the Philippians.

But whatever things were gain to me, those things I have counted as loss for the sake of Christ. More than that, I count all things to be loss in view of the surpassing value of knowing Christ Jesus my Lord, for whom I have suffered the loss of all things, and count them but rubbish so that I may gain Christ, and may be found in Him, not having a righteousness of my own derived from the Law, but that which is through faith in Christ, the righteousness which comes from God on the basis of faith. (Philippians 3:7–9 NASB-U)

Paul seems to be saying that there is a difference between religious activities, or in our case, Christian activities, and really *knowing* Jesus. He does not mean just knowing about God but a deep, intimate relationship.

The Big Five will naturally come out of knowing God, but they do not necessarily lead us to that knowledge. They are tools that only have value inasmuch as they are used for the right purpose.

Suppose I have a goal in life to build the greatest house ever built. To achieve that goal, I go to school and study every aspect of building, from design to construction. Then I work as an apprentice to a master builder and learn the tricks of the trade that you can't learn in school. Then I buy the best tools for building that money can buy.

There I stand, decked out with all the fancy tools and all the knowledge and skills to use them. But what good is any of that if I never build the house? There is no glory or value in the tools and knowledge in and of themselves.

I know many people who do the Big Five really well but do not really *know* God. But I don't know anyone who truly knows God who does not do the Big Five.

This principle is well defined in a book called *Refuel* by Doug Fields. I know many of you have been lost in the busyness of the Christian life yet feel like something is missing. Furthermore, you are filled with guilt about it. How can you work this hard at the Christian life and still feel so far from God? This short book will give new clarity to what it really means to spend refreshing time with God.

Refuel-Doug Fields
www.livingthatmattersbook.com/05.html

Why do so many miss the value that the most important thing in life is to truly know God in an intimate way? Why is it easier to get caught up in activity than to *"Cease striving and know that I am God?" (Psalms 46:10).* Part of the answer lies in understanding how Satan operates in our lives.

We know that Satan is responsible for a lot of pain in the world, but I do not think we understand why. In reality, Satan doesn't really care about you one way or the other. He doesn't care if you go to church or live a good or bad life. You mean nothing to him. Satan is consumed by his hatred of God and his belief that he should rightfully be God. His constant desire is not to hurt you but to hurt God. Since God's greatest desire is to have intimate fellowship with you, then the best way Satan can hurt God is to prevent that from happening. How does he do that?

Every time you move toward intimacy with God, Satan will bring pain into your life. The natural human response to pain is to pull away. In Luke 14:25–35, Jesus tells his followers that they need to count the cost of following Him. He gives an illustration of a king who goes to war with ten thousand men against an army of twenty thousand. He had to send a delegation to ask the terms of peace.

Many of you unknowingly have struck a deal with Satan for peace. Here are his terms: "I don't care if you go to church or in fact do any of the Big Five as long as you stay away from intimacy with God. If you stay clear of God, then I won't bother you." And that is where many live, busy with Christian activity but never really knowing God intimately.

Let's go back to Paul again. He felt so strongly about the difference between the Christian activity and every good thing in his life that he said this:

More than that, I count all things to be loss in view of the surpassing value of knowing Christ Jesus my Lord, for whom I have suffered the loss of all things, and count them but rubbish so that I may gain Christ. (Philippians 3:8 NASB)

The word translated here as *rubbish* is actually the slang word for excrement or manure. That is how strongly he felt about it. What seemed to cost him everything actually gained him the best thing. But he also understood that this choice would involve pain.

That I may know Him and the power of His resurrection and the fellowship of His sufferings, being conformed to His death. (Philippians 3:10 NASB-U)

Everyone would love to know the "power of His resurrection," the power that raised Jesus from the dead, but are we willing to pay the price of the "fellowship of His sufferings"? My friend, you will not know one without the other. But I promise you that when you experience this kind of relationship with the Creator of the universe, everything else in your life will pale in comparison.

I want to tell you that I am the happiest person I have ever known in my life. I know that is a bold statement, but many of my friends say the same thing about me. Why am I telling you this? It is because, as happy as I am, my life is full of pain. I suffer from chronic severe migraine and cluster headaches and debilitating arthritis. I am in constant physical pain. My life is about loving people. When you invest in people who are hurting, they will hurt you. I have been hurt deeply in my life.

My wife and I experienced four very painful miscarriages. When we first got married, we decided to let God choose when we would have children so we chose not to use birth control. (This is not because I think birth control is wrong.)

Six years later, still childless, we consulted doctors, who assured us everything was normal. We prayed and asked friends to pray that God would give us a child. When we got the news that my wife was pregnant, we gave glory to God for what we saw as a miracle. You can imagine our joy.

Several months later, our joy turned to sorrow when we lost that baby and I nearly lost my wife as well. I trusted God, but the pain was intense. I remember friends saying to me, "It's okay, God knows how you feel." Those words stung. That fact that God knew how I felt did not make me feel any better.

That night, after my wife fell asleep in the hospital, I went to the church and got on my knees at the altar to have it out with God. I told Him my life was His and He could do what He wanted with me, but I didn't understand how the fact that He knew how I felt would make me feel better.

God spoke something to my heart that changed me forever. He said, "Yes, it is true that I know how you feel. What you need to understand is that because of what you experienced today, just a little bit, you know how I feel." Could it be that on a small level I was feeling what God feels when someone dies not knowing him? I learned a part of God that day that I could not have known without pain. You can know joy in the midst of pain.

When I read these last few pages to my wife to see if the message was clear, her response was, "Now, if you do not tell them how to accomplish this, they will be frustrated. I hate to read books that tell me where I should be and don't tell me how to get there. Even though you are recommending some how-to books, they will want to know now."

I trust her wisdom and I understand that frustration, so in a moment I will share a little practical help to illustrate how to begin to have intimate fellowship with God. However, much guilt comes into our lives from striving to live right behavior when our values do not really support that behavior.

Before I give you practical help you need to know this. God said, ***"You will seek Me and find Me when you search for Me with all your heart" (Jeremiah 29:13 NASB).***

I once heard a story about one of the ancient Greek philosophers. It seems a young man had read the writings of this philosopher and decided he was the wisest man in the world. The young man wanted to follow him. The young man searched for the philosopher and found him standing by a river. He said, "I believe you are the wisest man in the world, and I want to know you. Will you teach me all that you know?"

Without hesitation, the philosopher grabbed the young man, threw him in the river, and held him under the water. The young man struggled but the philosopher was bigger and stronger. Knowing he was about to die and desperate for air, the young man's adrenaline kicked in. He was able to push the philosopher off and come to the surface, gasping for air.

When he finally caught his breath, he looked at the philosopher and said, "What is wrong with you? I say I want to know you, and you try to kill me. Why?"

The philosopher smiled and calmly said, "When you want to know me as badly as you wanted to get out of that water—then I will teach you."

If that is not truly your value—knowing God is everything, and wanting to know God more than you want to breathe—then all of the tools and practical applications for achieving this will become nothing more than another source of guilt and frustration.

Over thirty years ago, I read two books that truly opened my eyes to these spiritual values. One was *Lord Make My Life a Miracle* by Ray Ortlund. The other was *Practicing the Presence of God*, written in the fifteenth century by a monk named Brother Lawrence. After reading them, I began my journey to truly know God.

I often hear people pray something like this: "Lord, please be with me today." That prayer makes no sense. God lives within us and is with us twenty-four hours a day.

We really should be praying, "Lord, please make me aware of your presence today." This awareness doesn't come naturally.

We must literally practice the presence of God until we can say with Brother Lawrence, "For me the time of action does not differ from the time of prayer and in the noise and clatter of my kitchen, while several persons are calling for as many different things, I possess God in as great a tranquility as if I were upon my knees." ("The Practice of the Presence of God," compiled by Father Joseph de Beaufort, a collection of the wisdom and teachings of Brother Lawrence, a 17th century Carmelite monk)

I began a practice many years ago that is still changing me every day. It started with a little windup timer on a key chain that would buzz every fifteen minutes. Now I have a fancy watch that is set to sound an alarm randomly throughout the day. When the alarm sounds, a little message appears on the screen that says simply, "Holy God." When the alarm sounds, it is saying to me, "Are you aware that the presence of the holy God of the universe is with you right now?" I don't stop to pray or read my Bible or do anything. I just quietly acknowledge, "God is here."

This little practice has changed my life. I am driving down the freeway and some guy cuts me off. *Beep beep beep*: "Are you aware that the presence of the holy God of the universe is with you right now?" I am counseling with a couple who are screaming at each other. I am tired and have a headache and feel sorry for myself. *Beep beep beep*: "God is here."

It is always just the right timing, but after years of this it is ingrained in me. I am standing in line in a grocery store and my eye catches a racy picture on a magazine that I shouldn't be looking at. The thought suddenly pops into my head: "What if your God Clock goes off?" Simply being aware of His presence changes everything in your life.

When you become aware of His presence moment by moment, something else begins to happen. Nothing could be more awkward than two people spending the whole day together in silence. The awareness of His presence forces you to learn how to talk to Him, how to hear Him, and you begin to really know Him.

"My sheep hear My voice, and I know them, and they follow Me." (John 10:27 NASB)

"I am the good shepherd, and I know My own and My own know Me." (John 10:14 NASB)

Beep beep beep. As I was typing that last paragraph, my God Clock went off. "Thank you, Lord, for always being present with me." I could almost see Him smile and wink at me. I think He is pleased with what I have written. I think He is pleased you are reading it. He wants you to know Him.

Selah. This is a word seen often at the end of many of the Psalms. While we don't know the exact meaning, many scholars believe it means "stop and meditate on this."

This is what I would like you to do before reading the next section but after reading this excerpt from Ray Ortlund's book, Lord Make My Life a Miracle:

> "Yes, yes" you say hastily. "I accepted Christ when I was twelve, and that's already settled now let's go on to the Body, to fellowship, to work, to priorities, to lifestyle, to all these fun things everybody's chatting about these days."
>
> Wait! Stop! Be still! Be quiet!

You're nearsighted, my friend. Your eyes are focused on what's closest. So are the eyes of millions of other busy, nervous, frantic, activist Christians in this age.

Will you adjust your vision? Will you look beyond all that? Will you see the Lord, high and lifted up, seated on His throne, surrounded by worshiping Ones? Will you dare to lift your eyes?

You'll be smitten. You'll realize you're profane. You'll be separated from all your busy-busy, horizontally motivated brothers. You'll cry, "O God, my mouth is filthy, and I live among people with filthy mouths. I'm undone."

But oh, my friend! The sight of this Super Being will not crush you, but cleanse you. His fire will burn away all your filthiness, all your bitterness. (Yes I'm talking to Christians.)

You'll feel so free, so clean, so exhilarated that when you hear God's challenge for service that you'll be ready for ...

Number two: attention to the Body, and

Number three: attention to your work in this world. Don't rush past Number One. This is the blockbuster.

This, my Christian friend, may be your personal confrontation on the Damascus Road.

(Lord Make My Life a Miracle by Ray Ortlund, Gospel Light Publications 1974)

Sela.

Later, in chapter six, we will see how the financial values help to teach us to live this value.

Spiritual Value 2
We Are Designed to Be Part
of His Body, the Church

The value here, in truth, is that you cannot experience true, intimate fellowship with God and not desire that same fellowship with His family. To understand the profundity of this value, you must understand the three great loves of the Bible.

You might be thinking I am referring to the three Greek words in Scripture, all translated "love." I hear lots of teaching about that. First there is *eros*, from which we get the word *erotic*. This is primarily a physical love. Then there is *philo*, thought to be friendship or family love, as in Philadelphia: *philo* = love and *delphi* = brother, the city of brotherly love. The third is *agape*, said to be God's love or unconditional love. While this is an interesting comparison, these are not the three great loves to which I refer.

First, I want you to think about the amazing love between a father and son. But not just any father and son. I am talking about God the Father and God the Son. Sometimes in our passionate defense of the theology of the Trinity, we forget that though there is but one God, there are three distinct personalities in that Godhead who have a relationship to each other. This Father and Son have a bond of love beyond our understanding.

Proverbs 8:22–31 talks about a relationship between God and Wisdom. Many scholars believe that Wisdom there is really Jesus, and this describes their relationship. I happen to agree with that view. Look at this passage and see a beautiful story of a Son going to work with his Father and delighting Him as He works with Him.

"The Lord possessed me at the beginning of His way,
Before His works of old.
"From everlasting I was established,
From the beginning, from the earliest times of the earth.
"When there were no depths I was brought forth,
When there were no springs abounding with water.
"Before the mountains were settled,
Before the hills I was brought forth;
While He had not yet made the earth and the fields,
Nor the first dust of the world.
"When He established the heavens, I was there,
When He inscribed a circle on the face of the deep,
When He made firm the skies above,
When the springs of the deep became fixed,
When He set for the sea its boundary
So that the water would not transgress His command,
When He marked out the foundations of the earth;
Then I was beside Him, as a master workman;
And I was daily His delight,

> *Rejoicing always before Him,*
> *Rejoicing in the world, His earth,*
> *And having my delight in the sons of men.*
> *(Proverbs 8:22–31 NASB)*

At twelve years old, Jesus was already about His Father's business (Luke 2:49). Then, when he began His public ministry at the age of thirty, Jesus was baptized and a wonderful thing happened.

The Holy Spirit descended upon Him in bodily form like a dove, and a voice came out of heaven, "You are My beloved Son, in You I am well-pleased." (Luke 3:22 NASB)

I get the image of a father at a football game seeing his son score the winning touchdown. He can't help himself when he shouts out, "Hey, everybody, that's my son! Isn't he great?"

All through the book of John, Jesus loves to talk about His relationship with His Father, how He loves to imitate Him, and how His Father loves Him.

Therefore Jesus answered and was saying to them, "Truly, truly, I say to you, the Son can do nothing of Himself, unless it is something He sees the Father doing; for whatever the Father does, these things the Son also does in like manner. "For the Father loves the Son, and shows Him all things that He Himself is doing; and the Father will show Him greater works than these, so that you will marvel." (John 5:19–20 NASB)

The reason I want you to understand this love relationship between Father and Son is because, as much as they loved each other, they love you and I more. This is the second great love. Think about their relationship as you read again the most well-known verse in the Bible:

"For God so loved the world that He gave His only begotten Son, that whoever believes in Him shall not perish, but have eternal life." (John 3:16 NASB-U)

Their act of love for us caused them to be separated for the first time in eternity. In agony, the Son cried out, *"Eli, Eli, lama sabachthani?" that is, "My God, My God, why have You forsaken Me?" (Matthew 27:46 NASB-U)*

Why did they do all of this for us? Yes, of course, to pay for our sin that we may have eternal life. But there is more. Here comes that third great love. Read this amazing prayer that Jesus prayed for us in John 17:

Jesus spoke these things; and lifting up His eyes to heaven, He said, "Father, the hour has come; glorify Your Son, that the Son may glorify You, even as You gave Him authority over all flesh, that to all whom You have given Him, He may give eternal life. "This is eternal life that they may know You, the only true God, and Jesus Christ whom You have sent. "I glorified You on the earth, having accomplished the work which You have given Me to do. "Now, Father, glorify Me together with Yourself, with the glory which I had with You before the world was.

"I have manifested Your name to the men whom You gave Me out of the world; they were Yours and You gave them to Me, and they have kept Your word. "Now they have come to know that everything You have given Me is from You; for the words which You gave Me I have given to them; and they received them and truly understood that I came

forth from You, and they believed that You sent Me. "I ask on their behalf; I do not ask on behalf of the world, but of those whom You have given Me; for they are Yours; and all things that are Mine are Yours, and Yours are Mine; and I have been glorified in them. "I am no longer in the world; and yet they themselves are in the world, and I come to You. Holy Father, keep them in Your name, the name which You have given Me, that they may be one even as We are. "While I was with them, I was keeping them in Your name which You have given Me; and I guarded them and not one of them perished but the son of perdition, so that the Scripture would be fulfilled.

"But now I come to You; and these things I speak in the world so that they may have My joy made full in themselves. "I have given them Your word; and the world has hated them, because they are not of the world, even as I am not of the world. "I do not ask You to take them out of the world, but to keep them from the evil one. "They are not of the world, even as I am not of the world. "Sanctify them in the truth; Your word is truth. "As You sent Me into the world, I also have sent them into the world. "For their sakes I sanctify Myself, that they themselves also may be sanctified in truth.

"I do not ask on behalf of these alone, but for those also who believe in Me through their word; that they may all be one; even as You, Father, are in Me and I in You, that they also may be in Us, so that the world may believe that You sent Me.

"The glory which You have given Me I have given to them, that they may be one, just as We are one; I in them and You in Me, that they may be perfected in unity, so that the

world may know that You sent Me, and loved them, even as You have loved Me. "Father, I desire that they also, whom You have given Me, be with Me where I am, so that they may see My glory which You have given Me, for You loved Me before the foundation of the world.

"O righteous Father, although the world has not known You, yet I have known You; and these have known that You sent Me; and I have made Your name known to them, and will make it known, so that the love with which You loved Me may be in them, and I in them." (John 17:1–26 NASB)

In each place that He refers to "them" and "His own," you can literally insert your name because of verse twenty: *"I do not ask on behalf of these alone, but for those also who believe in Me through their word."* My friend, He is talking about you and me.

But it all boils down to the last verse: *"so that the love with which You loved Me may be in them, and I in them."* Yes; that third love is how we are to love each other.

"Just as the Father has loved Me, I have also loved you; abide in My love." (John 15:9 NASB-U)

It was His great sacrifice of love that compels us to love each other. *"And walk in love, just as Christ also loved you and gave Himself up for us, an offering and a sacrifice to God as a fragrant aroma." (Ephesians 5:2 NASB)*

"A new commandment I give to you, that you love one another, even as I have loved you, that you also love one another. "By this all men will know that you are My

disciples, if you have love for one another." (John 13:34–35 NASB-U)

There are many great resources for learning the mechanics of living out this relationship to the body of Christ. I want to mention two of them. First, I would highly recommend Eric Rees' book *S.H.A.P.E.* to help find your place in serving the body of Christ.

But as you know by now, this book is about values. It is our operating system. In his book *Building Up One Another*, Gene Getz examines the fifty-eight times in Scripture the words *one another* are used to exhort us toward twelve specific actions that really define how we are to love one another.

Before you go on to the next value, and before you try to figure out the how-to of life in the body of Christ, let this truly become your value:

"Since you have in obedience to the truth purified your souls for a sincere love of the brethren, fervently love one another from the heart." (1 Peter 1:22 NASB)

Sela.

Later, in chapter 6, we will see how the financial values teach us to live this value.

Spiritual Value 3
We Are Designed to Love the
World in His Name

To love the world in Jesus' name, you must see the world through His eyes.

And seeing the multitudes, He felt compassion for them, because they were distressed and downcast like sheep without a shepherd. Then He said to His disciples, "The harvest is plentiful, but the workers are few." "Therefore beseech the Lord of the harvest to send out workers into His harvest." (Matthew 9:36–38 NASB)

The word *compassion* here means that your internal organs ache from the intensity of the emotion that you feel. It wasn't just about "saving" them. They were like sheep without a purpose. They were so distressed that it broke His heart. His plan to reach them was us.

When you are living out the first two spiritual values, then this third value will be natural. You cannot know Him intimately and not know how much He loves the world. When you experience intimacy with God and with His family, people will notice. Remember what Jesus said?

"By this all men will know that you are My disciples, if you have love for one another." (John 13:34–35 NASB)

People will want what you have. They will ask. When they ask, you must be ready. Peter says it like this:

But even if you should suffer for the sake of righteousness, you are blessed. And do not fear their intimidation, and do not be troubled, but sanctify Christ as Lord in your hearts, always being ready to make a defense to everyone who asks you to give an account for the hope that is in you, yet with gentleness and reverence; and keep a good conscience so that in the thing in which you are slandered, those who revile your good behavior in Christ will be put to shame. (1 Peter 3:14–16 NASB)

Notice first that the opportunity to share the good news comes from suffering. It is how we respond to that suffering that makes people want what we have.

Conduct yourselves with wisdom toward outsiders, making the most of the opportunity. Let your speech always be with grace, as though seasoned with salt, so that you will know how you should respond to each person. (Colossians 4:5–6 NASB)

When you get the being before the doing, then the doing is easy. King David prayed a very famous prayer in Psalm 51 that is all about being:

> *Create in me a clean heart, O God,*
> *And renew a steadfast spirit within me.*
> *Do not cast me away from Thy presence,*
> *And do not take Thy Holy Spirit from me.*
> *Restore to me the joy of Thy salvation,*
> *And sustain me with a willing spirit.*
> *(Psalm 51:10–12 NASB)*

This is an amazing prayer of confession and repentance. David truly wants to know God and be right with Him. But you cannot fully understand the purpose of this prayer outside of the context of the next verse.

Then I will teach transgressors Thy ways,
And sinners will be converted to Thee.
(Psalm 51:13 NASB)

It was in knowing God intimately that David understood that he must bring others to that same relationship. David was a sinner, and he did some terrible things in his life. He violated God's design. As a result, he suffered a great deal of pain. But that pain drove him to God. Great was his sin, but greater was his heart for God.

The result is the book of Psalms, which gives great comfort in the midst of pain. This is the life that moves people toward a desire to know God. Psalms teaches us how to view God and how to relate to Him. It shows us how to express our discontent in the context of praise. But the most important result of experiencing the grace and forgiveness of God is a natural desire to share that with others. We become ambassadors for Christ.

Therefore, we are ambassadors for Christ, as though God were making an appeal through us; we beg you on behalf of Christ, be reconciled to God. (2 Corinthians 5:20 NASB)

Later, in chapter 5, we will see how the
financial values teach us to live this value.

How?

Selah ... now Selah some more ... still more ...

This first value category is too important to simply move on. What I am about to suggest may sound very strange, but remember I said in the beginning that this is not a book to be read once. It is to be studied over a lifetime. The best way to keep this in perspective is to reread this chapter again after each of the chapters that follow. Everything in the end should come full circle back to here. You will never be fully healthy in any of the categories until you are fully healthy in all of them.

....

Top Three Spiritual Values
(It's not about me; it's about God)

1. *We are designed for intimate fellowship with God.*

2. *We are designed to be part of His body, the church.*

3. *We are designed to love the world in His name.*

www.spiritualitythatmatters.com

Chapter 2 to be continued ...

CHAPTER 3

Relational Values

God's Design for Relationship

In each value category, I want to remind you again of the number one overarching value that governs all values:

It's not about you; it's about God.

If you do not believe that, then none of these values will make any sense to you.

I have had the experience of knowing some very wealthy people who, in spite of that wealth, are miserable. The reason that they are miserable is because their marriage is miserable. I have also known some very poor people who, in spite of their poverty, are happy and content. The reason they are happy and content is because their marriage is happy and content. I have also known wealthy people who are happy and content and poor people who are miserable. In most of those cases, the common denominator is the condition of their marriages.

I would submit to you that nothing in life affects whether we are miserable or content like our relationships with our spouses do. You can be in a great mood; then your spouse says one thing or gives you a certain look and your good mood is crushed. Other times you're discouraged or depressed. Just the right loving touch from your spouse and you begin to feel better.

This is part of the reason that I believe the two most important roles you will have in life are those of husband and father or wife and mother. Most people do not start preparing for these roles until six weeks before the wedding, in premarital counseling. I believe that most of what I am teaching in this book should be second nature by the time we are in our teens.

This chapter is not about how to make your marriage better. It is not even focused on giving you tools to fix your problems. It is about getting a perspective on how God designed the marriage relationship to work. When you finish the chapter, and if you agree that the values are biblically correct, then you will have to decide something. You are either living by this design or you are not. This is not something you take for a test drive to see if it works. If it is truly God's design, then you must commit to following it regardless of the perceived results.

If you try to apply these values before accepting that they are truly God's design, then you will view them in light of your experiences and culture and they will not make sense. Remember that your belief in the design will not determine whether it is true or not, but it will affect the way that you interact with it.

Relational Value 1
It's Not About Us; It's About God

Your marriage is no accident. God ordained and designed you and your spouse to be together. He has a purpose for your marriage that is greater than you. It's the same with individuals. I want you to know that this life is not about you. God has a greater purpose. I want you to see your marriage in a similar way.

I am addressing these statements to people who are already married. Before you are married, you do not know who God has ordained for you to be with. But you do not need to know. If you are not married, give up the notion of finding your "soul mate" or finding "the one." Unless you are a prophet, there is no such thing as "the one." You do not find a soul mate. You will spend a lifetime becoming soul mates with the person you marry. Make a decision in wisdom to marry someone who has godly character and shares your godly values, and that will be the person God has designed for you.

finding the right mate
www.livingthatmattersbook.com/06.html

If you understand that His purpose is greater than you, then it gives you a different motivation for wanting your marriage to be right. I have heard many statements like "I know divorce is wrong, but surely God would not want me to be unhappy," or "I made a mistake, but should I have to pay for it for the rest of my life"?

Marriage is not designed for your happiness. There is no doubt that when marriage is done according to God's design, you can be happy. But marriage's design is much greater than that. It will make you holy. It will make you more like Jesus.

Few people ever desire to get help or improve anything in their lives unless a relationship is affected. When people come to me for help, whether it is an addiction or another personal problem, almost always the reason they are there is because it has affected some relationship in their life, usually their marriages.

Marriage is like God's heavenly sandpaper. When you have a rough piece of wood and you want it to be smooth, you do not take rag and polish it. First you take a planer and tear away all the big, rough pieces. Then you take heavy-grit sandpaper that scratches and tears at the wood. You work your way down to finer and finer sandpaper as the wood gets smoother and smoother. Next you use very fine steel wool. The last step is maybe some wax or polish to make the wood shine. God uses your mate much the same way in your life.

When my wife and I met, we were as opposite as two people can be. We have both done extensive personality profiling. Each of our personality types is shared by only 4 percent of the population ... on the extreme opposite ends of the scale. I was the ADD poster child while she was OCD. Over nearly forty-four years together, God has whittled us down into a new creation. We think so much alike that often she speaks what I am thinking seconds before I have a chance to say it.

I never thought I would say this, but many of the behaviors that I used to dislike in my wife I now value as essential to our way of life. I credit her for every improvement in me.

It is in understanding this value that we will see two primary purposes for marriage. Later I will talk about how to discover God's unique purpose for your marriage, but I believe all marriages were designed for these two primary purposes.

After God had created all of the animals and then Adam, He made a very important declaration: *"It is not good for man to be alone."* He was not saying simply that Adam was lonely but that he was not created to be alone. This was not an afterthought of God's but rather His plan all along.

Then God said, "Let Us make man in Our image, according to Our likeness; and let them rule over the fish of the sea and over the birds of the sky and over the cattle and over all the earth, and over every creeping thing that creeps on the earth." God created man in His own image, in the image of God He created him; male and female He created them. (Genesis 1:26–27 NASB-U)

It is later, in Genesis 2, that we see the actual creation of the woman. Here in chapter 1, the narrative switches back and forth between singular and plural, male and female created in the image of God.

The reality is that a man by himself or a woman by herself is not the full reflection of the glory and image of God. When God joins male and female together, as one, then we have the complete reflection of the image of God. This is one of the primary purposes of marriage. Marriage brings together two parts of the same image, male and female.

If you notice, here God refers to Himself in the plural. This is not something He always does in Scripture, so I think there is a particular reason for it here. To fully reflect God the Father, God the Son, and God the Holy Spirit in relationship to each other requires relationship. It is through the roles of husband and wife played out by male and female that we fully reflect all that God is.

This is why the many attempts throughout the United States to redefine marriage are so vitally important to the way the universe works. Marriage exists to bring male and female together as one to be the reflection of the glory and image of God. This is accomplished in completeness through a man and a woman.

I have had many gay friends, and I love them. While I strongly disagree with their choice and do not support it in any way, I respect their legal right to make it. However, to define and practice marriage any other way than between a man and a woman violates God's design. It tears at the foundational building blocks for how God designed the universe to work.

Then the Lord God said, "It is not good for the man to be alone; I will make him a helper "suitable" for him." (Genesis 2:18 NASB)

The word *suitable* here literally means "opposite." This is not meant in a negative way but more like two sides to the same coin. Another good translation would be "corresponding to." This again is why it cannot refer to the same sex, because that would be two of the same part, not corresponding or opposite parts. These two parts were perfectly designed to fit together so that, as one, they could accomplish God's purposes.

Just as God made you uniquely different from all other human beings, He also made you and your mate to uniquely fit together in a way that no two other human beings can. Look at your mate. No matter how you feel about him or her right now, there is no other person who can complete the design and purpose God has for your marriage.

It is in this purpose that we begin to understand the roles of husband and wife. If these roles were created and designed to reflect the image of God, then how does that happen? How does marriage reflect the glory and image of God?

Husbands, love your wives, just as Christ also loved the church and gave Himself up for her, so that He might sanctify her, having cleansed her by the washing of water with the word, that He might present to Himself the church in all her glory, having no spot or wrinkle or any such thing; but that she would be holy and blameless. So husbands ought also to love their own wives as their own bodies. He who loves his own wife loves himself; for no one ever hated his own flesh, but nourishes and cherishes it, just as Christ also does the church, because we are members of His body. For this reason a man shall leave his father and mother and shall be joined to his wife, and the two shall become one flesh. This mystery is great; but I am speaking with reference to Christ and the church. (Ephesians 5:25–32 NASB)

I believe that one great purpose of the role of husband is to reflect the glory and image of God through the way he loves his wife. He is commanded to love her *as Christ loves the church*. This is why the Bible compares the relationship of husband and wife to the relationship of Christ and His church. As husbands model this in the church, the body of

Christ, then the church reflects this same love so all the world may see the love of God in the flesh.

God gives an amazing illustration of this value in the story of Hosea. Hosea was a prophet, and by God's instructions he married a prostitute named Gomer. Hosea fell in love with her and gave her a wonderful life, but she ran away and went back to her old life. Hosea pursued her and brought her home and forgave her. She ran away time and time again, and he forgave her every time. Finally she left him for another man, and he was heartbroken. He found out later that the man had left her and she was being sold as a slave on the auction block. In an incredible act of unconditional love, he bought her from the auction block and brought her home and forgave her.

This story is told in parallel with the story of God's relationship with His people. Israel was unfaithful to God, but God loved her and pursued her and forgave her. No wonder it was Hosea who preached to Israel, *"Come, let us return to the Lord. For He has torn us, but He will heal us. He has wounded us, but He will bandage us. He will revive us after two days; He will raise us up on the third day that we may live before Him. So let us know, let us press on to know the Lord. His going forth is as certain as the dawn; and He will come to us like the rain, Like the spring rain watering the earth"* (Hosea 6:1–3).

God used the marriage relationship of Hosea and Gomer to model His love for His people. This is still true of husbands today. Where we get into trouble is when we differ over how this love is manifested. There are expectations today that are not in harmony with a biblical view of love.

I believe that one great purpose of the role of wife is to reflect the glory and image of God through the way she respects and submits to her husband. She is commanded to submit to her husband *as unto the Lord*. I will talk more later in this chapter as to how these roles work in relationship to each other, but for now I want you to understand it in the context of God's purpose for marriage.

Now as the church submits to Christ, so also wives should submit to their husbands in everything. (Ephesians 5:24 NASB)

This shows clearly that the role of the wife is modeling how we relate to Christ. In other words, the way the church relates to Christ is the same as the way a wife relates to her husband.

It is relatively easy to see how a husband's love for his wife reflects God's image as he models God's love for us, and even how a wife's submission parallels how the church submits to Christ. But how does her submission reflect the image of God?

But I want you to understand that Christ is the head of every man, and the man is the head of the woman, and God is the head of Christ. (1 Corinthians 11:2 NASB)

But aren't God and Christ equal? How is God the head of Christ? God the Father, God the Son, and God the Holy Spirit are equal in essence. This means that all of the divine attributes are equally attributable to each of them. Attributes like omniscience, omnipresence, or unconditional love are true of all three persons of the Trinity. Together they are God.

However, as I stated in my discussion of spiritual values, in our defense of this fact, we often fail to recognize the differences. There is a definite order and structure to the Godhead. Jesus, though equal, is submitted to the Father. The Holy Spirit is submitted to the Son and the Father. The wife reflects this image of God in the way she submits to her husband.

Men and women are equal in essence. They are both heirs of the kingdom of God. They both have equal access as children of God to the throne of grace.

It is through this relationship of husband and wife that the world can see a practical demonstration of our relationship to God. I believe this is God's primary purpose in marriage. Through the way a husband and wife relate to each other, they model the relationship between God and His people. It truly reflects His glory and image.

This design and purpose was damaged when Adam and Eve fell. It was no longer a natural thing to reflect the image of God in the ways we have discussed. God said to Eve, "*Your desire will be for your husband, and he will rule over you.*"

These words mean that it would be the sinful desire of the woman to control her husband and the sinful desire of the husband to control his wife. God was telling them that in their sin, they would no longer naturally model the way God designed their relationship to be.

This does not mean, as some would say, that the roles of authority and submission are a result of the fall. Our difficulties in following those roles are a result of the fall. Thank God that He has restored us by His grace. It is only through that grace that we can once again reflect His image to the world.

The second purpose that God has for all marriages is also shown in Genesis. God told Adam and Eve to be fruitful and multiply. Multiply what? Of course it refers to offspring, but He was also telling them to reproduce the reflection of His image. In the case of Adam and Eve, it was because through their lineage the Messiah would come. The application for us is that we raise our children in the heritage of the Messiah.

It is very interesting how the Bible tells us about Adam's offspring: *"This is the book of the generations of Adam. In the day when God created man, He made him in the likeness of God, He created them male and female, and He blessed them and named them Man in the day they were created. When Adam had lived one hundred and thirty years, he became the father of a son in his own likeness, according to his image, and named him Seth"* *(Genesis 5:1–3 NASB).*

Saying that Seth was in Adam's likeness and according to his image does not mean the same thing as saying Adam was made in God's image. As I said earlier, Adam's likeness to God was damaged when Adam and Eve sinned. I like how Matthew Henry says it in his commentary: "This was Adam's own likeness, the reverse of that divine likeness in which Adam was made; but, having lost it himself, he could not convey it to his seed. A sinner begets a sinner, but a saint does not beget a saint." The beautiful part is that in naming Seth here rather than Abel (Abel was actually the firstborn), He is giving us a clue how, through the offspring of Adam and Eve, the Savior would come to restore that image.

"I will put enmity between you (Satan) and the woman, and between your seed and her seed; He shall crush you on the head and you shall bruise him on the heal." (Genesis 3:15 NASB)

Though it is not clearly stated in Scripture, I believe that Satan thought that lineage would come through the firstborn, Abel, so he tried to corrupt him. When he could not, Satan then corrupted Abel's brother Cain, who killed Abel.

But God had a different plan. It was to come through Seth, and that is why Seth is listed here.

Through that lineage, the Messiah came and paid the price of redemption. When our Redeemer left, He left behind His Spirit, who is in us, transforming us into His image.

[You] have put on the new self who is being renewed to a true knowledge according to the image of the One who created him. (Colossians 3:10 NASB)

But we all, with unveiled face, beholding as in a mirror the glory of the Lord, are being transformed into the same image from glory to glory, just as from the Lord, the Spirit. (2 Corinthians 3:18 NASB)

Just as through Adam's children came the lineage of the Redeemer who, by His Holy Spirit, is restoring us as image bearers, so we pass on through our children the heritage of reflecting that image to the world.

> *Unless the Lord builds the house,*
> *They labor in vain who build it;*
> *Unless the Lord guards the city,*

The watchman keeps awake in vain.
It is vain for you to rise up early,
To retire late,
To eat the bread of painful labors;
For He gives to His beloved even in his sleep.
Behold, children are a gift of the Lord,
The fruit of the womb is a reward.
Like arrows in the hand of a warrior,
So are the children of one's youth.
How blessed is the man whose quiver is full
of them;
They will not be ashamed
When they speak with their enemies in the gate.
(Psalm 127:1–5 NASB-U)

I believe this song by Solomon beautifully expresses how God views the importance of children to a marriage. Satan has propagated many myths about children. I hear them all the time. "We want to wait till we can afford it." "We want to take time for ourselves first to build our relationship before we have children." "I want to wait until I am more mature so I can be a good and wise parent."

As with most human thought, these concepts sound reasonable, but they are foreign to God's design and are simply not true. Studies show that families with children actually do better financially. How can you "build your relationship" properly when the purpose of that relationship is to reflect the image of God and multiply His family? The truth is that our bodies are designed to bear children in our youth. There are many health risks and emotional risks in later-life pregnancies.

One of the reasons these myths are believed is because often when marriages produce children early, they still miss their purpose. Couples do not live according to God's financial or spiritual values and have no understanding of relational or parental values. They become busy in labor to "provide for" and "protect" the family. That sounds right, doesn't it? But their efforts are often focused on the externals instead of investing in the children. This labor is in vain. It is a violation of God's design, yet once again we blame the design.

This song makes it clear that when we understand that children are a gift from God and have a purpose, we know that God will take care of provision and protection. In the chapter on parental values, we will examine the true purpose of children and how we fulfill that purpose. For now I simply want you to recognize this as God's value.

This principle has worked in spreading many belief systems for many generations. Catholicism doesn't grow from proselytizing; it grows from procreating. The same is true of Mormonism, Islam, and Communism: they all spread primarily through procreation. But it is not simply a matter of having many kids. The whole community is involved in raising them to be loyal to and serve their belief system. This even works with culture. There are some ethnic and culture groups that spread rapidly because of the numbers of children they have and the strong influence of culture in their upbringing.

Christianity has rebelled against this design. We have missed how God has always grown His people through procreation. Yes, we need spiritual procreation as well, i.e., bringing people to a new birth in Christ. But I believe we could saturate our land with Christianity in a few generations if we trusted

God's design in raising godly children. We will also see this design in chapter 5, about the sexual values.

Unfortunately, Satan understands this design all too well. While Christianity has forgotten this design, Satan has used it in America for his own gain. One of the reasons that we are so far out of design is that we have turned the education of our children over to everyone else but the home, where God says it should be. Generation after generation has been polluted by a humanist worldview. I will show this in more detail in chapter 4.

So the value is that it is not about us; it's about God! God has a purpose for our marriages that is bigger than us. I want to emphasize again that if this is not your value then the other relational values will not make sense.

Relational Value 2
The Roles of Husband, as Played by Man, and Wife, as Played by Woman, Reflect God through Authority and Submission

For the husband is the head of the wife, as Christ also is the head of the church, He Himself being the Savior of the body. (Ephesians 5:23 NASB)

But I want you to understand that Christ is the head of every man, and the man is the head of the woman, and God is the head of Christ. (1 Corinthians 11:2 NASB)

Authority and submission are critical in the reflecting of God's image and glory because that is the nature of the Godhead. We see this all through creation. The earth is in submission to the sun. If the earth were to get out of submission to the sun, it would have a catastrophic result. The moon is in submission to the earth. If it were to get out of submission, the result would again be bad.

We not only see this in the grandeur of creation but in the smaller elements. Inside of an atom is a nucleus. The electrons are in submission to the nucleus. If they were to get out of submission, we would have yet another catastrophic result. The role of the husband is the role of authority, and the role of the wife is the role of submission. In marriage, without authority and submission, there will be a catastrophic result.

God ordained, by His sovereign will, that the role of husband would be fulfilled by a man and that the role of wife would be fulfilled by a woman, and that through these roles His image would be reflected. Did He do this because a man was better suited to be a husband and a woman was better suited to be a wife? It may surprise you that I believe the answer is no. It is the other way around.

Because God decided that the role of the husband would be filled by a man, He then designed man with all of the tools necessary to fill that role. He did the same with woman. I know this may seem like semantics, but it makes an important distinction. Think about this. Can a man do the role of a wife? Can a woman do the role of a husband? Yes in both cases. Does this mean that they should? No.

I can walk on my hands. It is not very pretty and it is not very effective and I cannot keep it up for very long, but I can do it. My hands were not made to walk on any more than my feet were made to grasp things. I can do it, but God gave me two feet that are so much better designed for that purpose. The sad thing is that walking on my hands eventually has a negative effect on my entire body. When a man and woman try to fill roles they were not designed to fill, it affects the whole family in a negative way.

There is no better example of this than Adam and Eve. When Adam abdicated his role and Eve stepped into his role, it left her wide open to a satanic attack that she was not designed to handle. The result not only affected them but all of humanity.

With this in mind, we can get clue as to what the roles of the husband and wife are by examining the tools that God gave them. In other words, we need to understand how God designed a man and how He designed a woman.

If we see a man on the street and he has a tool belt around his waist and is carrying a skill saw, it might be safe to assume that he builds things. We assume this because we know that building is the purpose of these tools. If we see a woman wearing scrubs and a stethoscope around her neck, we may assume she works in the medical field, because that is the purpose of those tools.

We live in a society that wants to believe that men and women are the same and therefore their roles are the same, or at least interchangeable. We are very confused even among Christians as to what it means to be a man or a woman, and therefore we are just as confused about the roles of husband and wife.

If we examine the way that men and women are designed physically and emotionally, it gives a hint as to the tools they are given to fulfill their roles. I do not want to speak inappropriately here, but I think you can get what I mean. Women are designed to be sensitive and open to the world and to receive the world unto themselves. Men are designed to penetrate their world and to surround and protect it. (More on this in chapter 5.)

Sometimes, when I am teaching on this subject, I ask the women in the crowd to describe for me the ideal mate. As I write their answers on the board, they say things like, "He should be a good listener, understanding. He should be sensitive to my needs and think about me first." Most of the answers are of this nature. These are all wonderful qualities.

Then I ask the women, "Let's say you find a man who has all of these qualities and more. Not only that, but he looks like Brad Pitt. He just has this one fault. He has never had a job and never intends to. He wants to stay home and watch the kids while you work to support the family. How many of you would that take him off of your list?" Almost every time, nearly every hand goes up.

Men are raised believing that what it means to be a man and a good husband is to simply be a good provider. This is what a man has been trained to do. Then he gets married and finds out all of these other things he is supposed to be and was never trained to do.

Along with that, men receive a deceptive message hundreds of times a day from hundreds of sources. They see it on television and in movies. They read it on billboards and in magazines. The subtle message is that what it really means to be a man is to have sex with as many beautiful women as he can before he dies. We are led to believe that this is the way a man is wired and he has no control over it. (I will have much to say about this in the chapter on sexual values.) No wonder men are so confused.

Women are just as confused. Women today are caught between two generations of teaching and value systems. On one side, they are told that all you really need in life as a woman is to find the right man. Everything else will fall into place. On the other side, they are told that not only does a woman not need a man, but men are responsible for every bad thing in women's lives.

Remember when I asked the women to describe the ideal mate? If you could see everything written on that board, you would find that it is really a description of a woman. No wonder so many teenage girls describe themselves as lesbian or bisexual. If we are to understand the roles of husband and wife, we must first embrace the value that though male and female are spiritually equal in God's eyes, they are very different in function and roles. "Vive la différence."

I believe that we are designed and created with a need to fully express our sexual identities—our maleness and femaleness. That is best done when male and female are *"of the same mind, maintaining the same love, united in spirit, intent on one purpose" (Philippians 2:2).*

In marriage, we do not lose our sexual identities; we fulfill them. It is in the roles of husband and wife that we truly live according to our design as men and women. Men are uniquely and exclusively designed to be husbands. They are given all the tools necessary for that role. Women are uniquely and exclusively designed to be wives. They are given all the tools necessary for that role.

This brings up and interesting point. It amazes me how often men want to tell women how to be wives, something about which men know nothing. Women want to tell men how to be husbands, something about which they know nothing. Philippians 2:2 works because when we yield our rights to God, then our desire is not to control our mates but, in mutual submission, to help them to live according to their design.

The Role of Husband

What then is the role of a husband? We have already shown that the primary role of the husband is to model God's love through the way he loves his wife. To have a complete understanding of the role, we must understand the position of the role.

For the husband is the head of the wife, as Christ also is the head of the church, He Himself being the Savior of the body. (Ephesians 5:23 NASB-U)

But I want you to understand that Christ is the head of every man, and the man is the head of a woman, and God is the head of Christ. (1 Corinthians 11:3 NASB-U)

The fact that the husband is the head of the house is clearly shown in Scripture, but what that means can be confusing. This is not an issue of equality but of function. I believe that the husband has 100 percent authority over his wife and family and for a very good reason. He is also given 100 percent of the responsibility.

In the garden of Eden, when Adam and Eve ate the forbidden fruit, God came first to Adam. Adam was responsible, not only for his actions, but also for those of Eve.

It was Eve who first ate and gave the fruit to Adam.

When the woman saw that the tree was good for food, and that it was a delight to the eyes, and that the tree was desirable to make one wise, she took from its fruit and ate; and she gave also to her husband with her, and he ate. (Genesis 3:6 NASB-U)

But the New Testament only speaks of Adam's sin, which brought death into the world.

Nevertheless death reigned from Adam until Moses, even over those who had not sinned in the likeness of the offense of Adam, who is a type of Him who was to come. (Romans 5:14 NASB-U)

For as in Adam all die, so also in Christ all will be made alive. (1 Corinthians 15:22 NASB-U)

Adam was given authority over his wife because he was given full responsibility. That authority was not a dictatorship. He was responsible for protecting his family. When Adam did not fulfill his role and Eve stepped outside of his authority, she also stepped outside of his protection and exposed herself to a danger she was not designed to face.

And it was not Adam who was deceived, but the woman being deceived, fell into transgression. (1 Timothy 2:14)

This verse is often used to point out the weakness of the woman and even to blame her for the sin in the garden. In fact it is an indictment against Adam. The woman was deceived and yielded to the temptation. Adam was not deceived at all. He knew exactly what was going on and stood there and watched it happen.

It makes me think about how an older sibling might prod his younger brother to go sneak some candy out of the candy jar. Then, when the younger brother gets caught with the candy, the elder says innocently, "I didn't do it. Johnny gave me the candy."

The biblical concept of authority focuses not on ruling, but on protecting. Jesus was given authority over all men, but what did that mean? How did He use His authority? It was for protection. The primary purpose and role of any authority is protection. This is how husbands are to use their authority.

For the husband is the head of the wife, as Christ also is the head of the church, He Himself being the Savior of the body. (Ephesians 5:23 NASB)

Let's look again at the prayer of Jesus in John 17 and see His attitude about His authority.

"Even as You gave Him authority over all flesh, that to all whom You have given Him, He may give eternal life." (John 17:2 NASB)

"While I was with them, I was keeping them in Your name which You have given Me; and I guarded them and not one of them perished but the son of perdition, so that the Scripture would be fulfilled." (John 17:12 NASB)

"I do not ask You to take them out of the world, but to keep them from the evil one." (John 17:15 NASB)

He was protecting us and guarding us and praying for our protection from Satan. Men, do you use your authority to protect your family or to lord it over them like a dictator? Are you a tool of God to fight Satan on behalf of your family, or are you a tool of Satan to enslave your family? Look at the contrast in these verses.

Husbands, love your wives and do not be embittered against them. Children, be obedient to your parents in all things, for this is well-pleasing to the Lord. Fathers, do not exasperate your children, so that they will not lose heart. (Colossians 3:19–21 NASB)

If your family is bitter and angry, it is a sure bet you do not understand the biblical view of authority. Godly authority is love. It is sacrifice. It is guarding your family to present them holy before God.

Husbands, love your wives, just as Christ also loved the church and gave Himself up for her, so that He might sanctify her, having cleansed her by the washing of water with the word, that He might present to Himself the church in all her glory, having no spot or wrinkle or any such thing; but that she would be holy and blameless. So husbands ought also to love their own wives as their own bodies. He who loves his own wife loves himself; for no one ever hated his own flesh, but nourishes and cherishes it, just as Christ also does the church, because we are members of His body. (Ephesians 5:25–30 NASB)

This is the true value of authority: to love and protect your wife and family as Christ did His church.

These then are the two major components of the role of husband: he is the spiritual leader, and he is to love his wife, reflecting the image of God.

Let's examine now what it means to be the spiritual leader.

I have interviewed many Christian women with this question: "What is your greatest wish for your husband?" The number one response is a wish to be loved. But a great number of them also say they wish their husbands would become spiritual leaders in their homes. When I ask what that means, most of the answers cover the same things: "I wish he would pray more and read his Bible." "I wish he would be more of a Christian example to our kids." "I wish he had a greater passion for God."

While these things describe a godly man (and for that matter a godly woman), they do not necessarily describe a spiritual leader. These are things all men should be. They are things all women should be as well.

Being a spiritual leader goes beyond these things. It is the same role that a pastor fills over the church. I believe that it involves two basic functions. First, as the spiritual leader, the husband is to cast the vision for where the family is going and what its purpose is. In this value category we are covering two major purposes that I believe God has for all marriages but I believe that he has very specific purposes for each individual marriage. It is the role of the spiritual leader to identify the purposes God has for the marriage and to lead his family in that direction.

I have heard a lot of teaching about what causes women to be insecure. It is said that when the husband is not being a responsible provider, his wife will be financially insecure. If he is not showing her love and affection, she will be relationally insecure. I believe, however, that the greatest source of insecurity in a family is when the members do not understand the purpose and significance of their family. I believe women and children can bear many hardships, whether financial, relational, or others, if they have a strong understanding of their purpose as a family.

The second task of the spiritual leader comes from the first. The husband must identify his family's shape. Earlier I recommended a book by Erik Rees called *S.H.A.P.E.* This is an acrostic that stands for spiritual gifts, heart passion, abilities, personality type, and experiences. These are the things that make us unique as individuals and define how we might best serve the body of Christ.

Just as each individual has a unique shape, so does each family. The spiritual leader must identify this shape and how it defines the way his family will fulfill the vision and purpose he has cast.

Let me be clear: this is simply a tool of understanding rather than a theological mandate. The Bible says nothing about "finding your shape." This is a principle gleaned from lots of Scripture passages about who we are in Christ and then applying it to the family.

It is also true that the role of the husband is one of provider. Scripture makes it very clear. In fact, Paul tells Timothy that a man who does not provide for his family is worse than an unbeliever. Why has this task been given to the husband?

Again we must look to the purpose of marriage to understand our roles. The husband is modeling how God relates to us, thereby reflecting His image.

It is vital, in order to fulfill the role of husband, that a man is a diligent student of God's Word. He is to be the primary disciple and teacher of his family. When Satan tempted Eve in the garden of Eden, purposely misquoting God, she did not know the right answer. She in turn also misquoted God. The reason she did not know is because Adam had not properly taught her. The truth is that from what we see in Scripture, God did not give the command to Eve. He gave it to Adam before Eve was even created. This why Paul told Timothy that it was the woman who was deceived, not the man. It was Adam's fault that she was deceived.

My wife attended Women's Bible Study Fellowship for many years. During that time she studied most of the major books and concepts of the Old and New Testaments. She spent thirty weeks on each course. After several years, participants receive a Bible education comparable to many seminary degrees. Thousands of women are getting this education.

Men! *Step up!* It is time for us to become no less diligent in our pursuit of biblical knowledge. I would encourage you to start with a basic catechism, which you will find in the next chapter. And I highly recommend that you become an expert at Proverbs.

Be diligent to present yourself approved to God as a workman who does not need to be ashamed, accurately handling the word of truth. (2 Timothy 2:15)

The demise of men
www.livingthatmattersbook.com/07.html

The Role of Wife

We have already shown that the primary role of the wife is to reflect the image of God and model the way we relate to God through her submission to her husband. As with the husband, in order to have a complete understanding of the wife's role, we must first understand the position.

Then the Lord God said, "It is not good for the man to be alone; I will make him a helper suitable for him." (Genesis 2:18 NASB)

It was not just a matter of Adam being lonely. He was not complete. We stated earlier in the chapter that the word *suitable* in the Hebrew means "opposite" or "corresponding to." God did not create the woman as an afterthought. Remember that God sees spouses as one because He created them as one. He had designed all along for male and female to be joined together as one in a beautiful reflection of His image.

God created and designed the woman to be a helper to the man. That is her position or role. Many women are uncomfortable with the concept of being a helper. It sounds like an inferior position. But the word here, *ezer*, translated "helper," is primarily used in Scripture in reference to God. I don't think we could say that God is inferior. The position of helper is a position of honor.

Wives be subject to your husbands, as to the Lord
For the husband is the head of the wife, as Christ also is the head of the church, He Himself being the Savior of the body.
Now as the church submits to Christ, so also wives should submit to their husbands in everything. (Ephesians 5:22–24)

Notice that the submission is *as to the Lord*. A wife is to submit to her husband in the same way she submits to the Lord. We do not consider submitting to the Lord as a bad thing. It is a joy.

Submission has become a bad word in our culture. I think I understand why. For many years and in many cultures, women have been mistreated. The concept of authority, being rooted more in protection than ruling, has not been understood. This was no more the way God designed it to be than the opposite extreme we find in our culture today, where we have rejected the whole idea of submission and authority.

I am old enough (and drug-free enough) to remember the sixties and what has been called the Women's Liberation Movement. Women joined together to protest "male domination." The symbol of this movement was the burning of bras. Women saw the bra as a symbol of a male-dominated society.

The original women's liberation movement actually started in Corinth two thousand years ago. In that time, the symbol of authority was a head covering. Women were required to cover their heads in church as a sign that they were under authority. Some women in Corinth stopped wearing their head coverings, and it became an issue in the church. In essence their refusal to cover their heads was like burning the bra.

In 1 Corinthians 11, Paul addresses this issue. I should point out that there are some Bible scholars who believe that the "head covering" was not a physical piece of clothing but rather the length of the hair. A woman's long hair was considered cover her head. Either way, the issue is the same. Paul is teaching about the principle and design of authority and submission more than the symbol.

He starts the chapter by defining the authority structure of the universe.

But I want you to understand that Christ is the head of every man, and the man is the head of a woman and God is the head of Christ. (1 Corinthians 11:3 NASB)

This is the point of the chapter. This is what they were rebelling against. This passage is not just about the women. The men did clearly not understand the proper place of authority. Women of that time were treated like property. The authority that men had was not theirs because they were superior and not simply because they were men. It was given by God because of the role men were to play in context of the whole chain of authority.

For a man ought not to have his head covered, since he is the image and glory of God; but the woman is the glory of man. (1 Corinthians 11:7 NASB)

Remember that this is all about reflecting the image of God. Neither man nor woman can do this alone. It is in the proper place of submission and authority that we truly reflect His image and glory.

For man does not originate from the woman, but the woman from man;
For indeed man was not created for the woman's sake but the woman for the man's sake.
Therefore the woman ought to have a symbol of authority on her head. (1 Corinthians 11:8–10 NASB)

The bottom line here is that a wife cannot pray as God intended outside of the structure of authority. But this is not some inferior position or punishment. It is just as true that a husband cannot pray when he is not fulfilling the proper design for authority. (We will see that clearly in 1 Peter a little later)

Let me be perfectly clear. This is not an issue of equality but purely of position. The next two verses bring it into focus.

However, in the Lord, neither is woman independent of man, nor is man independent of woman.
For as the woman originates from the man, so also the man has his birth through the woman; and all things originate from God. (1 Corinthians 11:11–12 NASB)

It is through interdependence that we live as one the way God designed it to be. Let me come full circle back to that value that God sees us as one and look at some verses that clearly show this position of authority and submission.

First, let's look again at what it looks like when we are living and relating according to God's design. Remember back in chapter 1 under Yielding Your Rights to God?

Make my joy complete by being of the same mind, maintaining the same love, united in spirit, intent on one purpose. (Philippians 2:2 NASB)

This is only accomplished through living according to God's design.

Now I want to examine how seriously God takes the positions of authority and submission. The passages I want to look at come from 1 Peter 2:13–3:7.

Submit yourselves for the Lord's sake to every human institution, whether to a king as the one in authority or to governors as sent by him for the punishment of evildoers and the praise of those who do right.

Here is another example that authority is about protection. That is the primary purpose of government, just as it is the primary purpose for all authority.

For such is the will of God that by doing right you may silence the ignorance of foolish men.
Act as free men, and do not use your freedom as a covering for evil, but use it as bondslaves of God.

We cringe at the thought of the word *slavery*. We understandably only see it in a negative light. But Jesus said if you want to be first in His kingdom, you will be the slave of all. (This is not forced slavery, which should always be condemned.) He then demonstrated that with His life (Mark 10:43–45).

This is a critical point in understanding the true position of submission for a wife. It is absolutely vital that in order for it to reflect the image of God, this submission *must* be voluntary. Remember, her submission is to be "as the church submits to Jesus Christ." God created us with the choice to serve Him or not. In order for a woman to reflect this, her submission must also be by choice.

Just as a husband's love must reflect the unconditional love of God, which is undeserved, so the wife's submission must be by choice, even when unearned by her husband. Look at these next verses.

Servants, be submissive to your masters with all respect, not only to those who are good and gentle, but also to those who are unreasonable.
For this finds favor, if for the sake of conscience toward God a person bears up under sorrows when suffering unjustly.
For what credit is there if, when you sin and are harshly treated, you endure it with patience? But if when you do what is right and suffer for it you patiently endure it, this finds favor with God.

Jesus was God and yet, as we showed earlier, He did not hold on to that. He freely submitted Himself to authority.

Look what the result was. He was treated horribly. He set the example.

For you have been called for this purpose, since Christ also suffered for you, leaving you an example to follow in His steps.
Who committed no sin, nor was any deceit found in His mouth;
and while being reviled, He did not revile in return; while suffering, He uttered no threats, but kept entrusting Himself to Him who judges righteously;
and He himself bore our sins in His body on the cross, so that we might die to sin and live to righteousness; for by His wounds you were healed.
For you were continually straying like sheep, but now you have returned to the Shepherd and Guardian of your souls.

Notice how it ends. The result of submission is security under protection of authority, i.e., *the Shepherd and Guardian of your souls*.

As we move into chapter 3, we see how this all applies to the roles of husband and wife.

In the same way, you wives, be submissive to your own husbands so that even if any of them are disobedient to the word, they may be won without a word by the behavior of their wives.
as they observe your chaste and respectful behavior.

Notice that it does not say, "Women, submit to men." As we have said before, this is not an issue of equality between men and women. This is about the position and roles of husbands and wives. Wives are not told to submit to *all men* but rather to their *own husbands*. It is also very clear that submission is not earned by the husband. It is given in reflection of Christ, according to His example.

All of this places the wife in a very vulnerable position. Look at the illustration that is given in verse 6:

"Just as Sarah obeyed Abraham, calling him lord, and you have become her children if you do what is right without being frightened by fear."

This verse refers, in part, to an amazing story of submission. Abraham and Sarah were traveling. When they met up with King Abimelech, Abraham was afraid and told the king that Sarah was his sister. She did not protest or contradict her husband. In fact, she went along with it and said Abraham was her brother. She went willingly as the king took her away.

But God intervened and warned the king that she was really Abraham's wife. God said that if Abimelech touched her, God would bring judgment on him. What God actually said was, "I did not let you touch her."

What an amazing story of submission. It was truly "as unto the Lord." What makes it even more amazing is that this didn't just happen once but twice. Each time God intervened and protected Sarah. She did not show any fear. The Bible says that you are her child if you do what is right without fearing.

It is very important that we understand the depth of what verse 6 is teaching us. The theme of doing right is repeated throughout the letter and is often accompanied by examples of suffering.

Hold On a Minute, Husbands!

This chapter is not here just to teach wives to be submissive. It is about the connection and unity that come from the union of submission and authority. There is a reason for this union that we will see soon. First, let's talk about the authority.

You husbands in the same way, live with your wives in an understanding way, as with someone weaker, since she is a woman; and show her honor as a fellow heir of the grace of life, so that your prayers will not be hindered. (1 Peter 3:7 NASB)

Men, this is where the rubber meets the road. God has given you an incredible responsibility. The words "in an understanding way" are better translated "according to knowledge." It is not just being understanding of your wives, though you certainly should be. It is really in understanding what marriage is all about—*submission and authority reflecting the image of God*—that you can live with your wife in an "understanding way." As with the wives, he tells the husbands "in the same way."

In the same way as what? The same way the previous chapter just taught us about submission and authority. God has designed your wife to be vulnerable. The passages we examined from 1 Peter certainly teach us the vulnerability of submission. He designed you, as husband, to protect that vulnerability.

We have already discussed the design of authority and submission in reflecting God's image. We also discussed how God uniquely designed male and female to fit those roles and then gave us clues in our physical design. There is reference to that here regarding the woman being the "weaker vessel." She is not inferior. She is vulnerable.

You are not her king. You are her protector. Be a man of "safety." (Reference the vows shown later in the chapter.) Show her honor as a daughter of God.

Husbands
www.livingthatmattersbook.com/08.html

The story of Esther gives a beautiful illustration of how God works through a truly submissive wife. King Ahasuerus (sometimes called Xerxes) was a powerful and, in many ways, wicked ruler. Esther was forced to become his bride, but she chose to love and submit to him, believing that to do so was serving God. She truly understood this was "not about her." ("I was born for such a time as this.")

Because of this, the king fell in love with her. Through her submission, she was able to expose an evil plot to destroy God's people, the Jews. But it seemed too late. The order had already been given by the king, and even he could not revoke it.

Esther could have become angry and told the king how stupid he was and how he would pay for harming God's chosen people. Instead, she humbly and in full submission to his will offered an alternative. The king saw her wisdom and granted her request. It saved the Jews from sure annihilation.

Melding the Roles Together

I hope you can see that authority and submission are not the same as superior and inferior. It is only when these roles work together in harmony that we can really see that.

I want to take yet another look at what I believe is a biblical definition of these roles—or, for that matter, any relationship—working in harmony.

Make my joy complete by being of the same mind, maintaining the same love, united in spirit, intent on one purpose. (Philippians 2:2 NASB)

Remember that these roles are "corresponding" or complementary to one another. They are to be completely interdependent. It is in that interdependence we see again it is not about us. It's about God.

However, in the Lord, neither is woman independent of man, nor is man independent of woman. For as the woman originates from the man, so also the man has his birth through the woman; and all things originate from God. (1 Corinthians 11:11–12 NASB)

I hope this will be evident in the Vows for Husbands and Wives on the following pages. I encourage you to memorize them and meditate on them daily. If you do, I believe you will be on your way to living out Philippians 2:2 in your marriage.

I want to make you a ninety-day challenge. For ninety days, memorize and meditate on the vows. Saturate your brain so deeply with these vows that they will be like a song you cannot get out of your head. Do not focus on acting out the vows. (Do not resist it either.) Simply let the Holy Spirit renew your mind into believing that this is your design as husband or wife.

It is important to note that a husband cannot fully understand his vows apart from the vows for wives, and a wife cannot fully understand her vows apart from the vows for husbands.

I encourage you to go to: www.livingthatmatters.com under the resources tab select downloads then download the vows and put copies everywhere. Then go to the link below and watch these videos.

ninety day challenge
www.livingthatmattersbook.com/09.html

These videos will explain in detail the meaning of these vows. I encourage you to watch them several times over the course of the ninety-day challenge. It will further help to engrain the vows on your brain.

These vows are extracted primarily from the following verses, along with many more too numerous to list: Genesis 1–3; 1 Corinthians 11:1–12;

Ephesians 5:22–33; Titus 2:1–8; 1 Peter 2:13–25; 3:1–7; 1 Corinthians 13:1–13, and 1 John 1–5.

Vows for Husbands
To be a ...

Spiritual

Man of Faith: to truly live in a way that makes clear to everyone, "It's not about me. It's about God."

Man of Prayer: to pray boldly in ways that tangible, measurable results happen in our lives every day.

Man of Action: to be a doer of the Word, knowing His Word and then obeying, no matter how difficult it may be.

Personal

Man of Integrity: to live my life above reproach, leaving Satan no room for blackmail. When everything I say matches everything I do.

Man of Honor: to place doing right above being right, revealing the character of God through my life. I am not a man of honor unless you say I am.

Man of Dignity: to leave a legacy and example that our children can be proud of, living humbly, becoming worthy of your respect.

Relational

Man of Love: to love you in a way that reflects the glory and image of God, as Christ loves the church and as my own body. May my very acts of love make you a woman of virtue.

Man of Vision: to be a leader you can follow, firm but flexible, clear but unexplainable, confident but humble. May my very acts of leadership and vision make you a woman of purpose.

Man of Safety: to use my authority to fight diligently to free you from all physical, emotional, mental, and spiritual bondage. To be your knight in shining armor. May my very acts of safety free you to be a woman of beauty.

Vows for Wives
To be a ...

Spiritual

Woman of Faith: to truly live in a way that makes it clear to everyone, "It's not about me. It's about God."

Woman of Prayer: to partner with you in agreement to "loose and bind," according to Matthew 18:18–19.

Woman of Action: to partner with you to be a doer of the Word, knowing His Word and then obeying, no matter how difficult it may be.

Personal

Woman of Virtue: to live my life above reproach, leaving Satan no room for blackmail. To live with moral excellence and modesty in body, mind, and spirit.

Woman of Purpose: to be a husband lover and a children lover, managing our household under your authority. I am not a woman of purpose if it does not fulfill your vision.

Woman of Beauty: to reflect outwardly, through appearance and conduct, the gentle, quiet reverence of my heart for God.

Relational

Woman of Respect: to show you honor and respect "as unto the Lord." To submit to you as the church does to Jesus. May my very acts of my respect make you a man of honor.

Woman of Help: to help you fulfill your God-given vision: showing understanding when it is not understandable, conforming when it is not comfortable, humble when it seems humiliating. May my very acts of help make you a man of integrity.

Woman of Encouragement: to give nurture, healing, and comfort as you fight as a warrior for my safety. May my very acts of encouragement make you a man of dignity.

Relational Value 3
God Sees You as One and Divorce
Is Not Part of His Design

When I do a wedding, I always start out by announcing to the guests that they have come today to witness a true miracle. After the exchanging of vows and rings, I kneel with the couple and ask God to do what I cannot do. He takes two people and makes them one. This is a miracle. Much like the birth of a baby and the new birth we experience when Christ comes into our lives for the first time (1 Corinthians 5:17), marriage creates a brand-new entity.

"So they are no longer two, but one flesh. What therefore God has joined together let no man separate." (Matthew 19:6 NASB)

I believe this is more than just a commandment. It is a statement of fact. Because only God can perform the miracle of two becoming one, it is only God who can tear it apart. This is why divorce is so painful. It is like severing a limb from the body. It must be your value that God designed marriage to be a permanent union and that divorce is not an option.

I know many of you will be thinking, "What about the cases of adultery or abuse?" First, I do not believe anyone should live with physical abuse. While it is not given as biblical grounds for divorce, you should not live in an unsafe place.

The term "emotional abuse" is used a lot in our society today. The problem is that the concept of emotional abuse is subjective. It is applied to everything from "he/she hurt my feelings" to "he/she just wants to control me." How these things affect us is determined by our backgrounds, our personal language differences, and many other variables. Often if we have truly yielded our rights to God and we are allowing God to meet our needs, these same things will not be able to "abuse" us.

I am not saying that there is no such thing as emotional abuse. The Bible teaches very clearly that words can have as severe a damaging effect as physical abuse. I have observed this in both men and women. Men tend to be very direct and cutting in their verbal abuse, while women tend to be more subtle and indirect. The result is the same. The damage is as real as being struck with a fist. The point we must remember is that although real abuse, whether physical or emotional, should never be tolerated, the Bible never gives "being a jerk" as grounds for divorce.

The Bible does give allowance for divorce in the case of unfaithfulness, but I do not believe this means what most people think. First of all, Jesus made it very clear that marriage was never designed to include divorce, under any circumstances.

Some Pharisees came to Jesus, testing Him and asking, "Is it lawful for a man to divorce his wife for any reason at all?" And He answered and said, "Have you not read that He who created them from the beginning made them male and female, and said, 'For this reason a man shall leave his father and mother and be joined to his wife, and the two shall become one flesh'? "So they are no longer two, but one flesh. What therefore God has joined together let no man separate." They said to Him, "Why then did Moses command to give her a certificate of divorce and send her

away?" He said to them, "Because of your hardness of heart Moses permitted you to divorce your wives; but from the beginning it has not been this way."(Matthew 19:3–8 NASB)

All of this makes it clear that divorce was not part of the original design. But people tend only to focus on the next verse:

"And I say to you, whoever divorces his wife, except for immorality, and marries another woman commits adultery." (Matthew 19:9 NASB)

I believe, along with many Bible scholars, that the word *immorality* is not talking about a single act of adultery. Rather, it refers to a continued, unrepentant pattern. That doesn't mean a single act of adultery is okay. But when there is true repentance, there can be healing. I have seen many marriages end up stronger than ever. In either case, divorce should be the last option, not the first.

Much more needs to be said about cases of abuse or unfaithfulness. However, for the purpose of this book, the value I want you to get is that God sees you as one, and God hates divorce.

I hope these videos can help clarify what the Bible says about divorce. While I do not agree with everything they say, my disagreements are minor and do not detract from their value.

MacArthur part one
www.livingthatmattersbook.com/10.html

MacArthur part two
www.livingthatmattersbook.com/11.html

How?

I could not possibly cover all of the relational values in this chapter. I would have to cover the entire Bible. But this is a good start. Let me repeat what I said at the beginning of the chapter:

When you finish the chapter, and if you agree that the values are biblically correct, then you will have to decide something. You are either living by this design or you are not. This is not something you take for a test drive to see if it works. If it is truly

God's design, then you must commit to following it regardless of the perceived results.

So what is your decision? If it is as I hope, then start with the vows and the ninety-day challenge presented in the video and then move forward to parental values. Those vows will be your foundation for the parental values. Each chapter in turn sheds new light on the previous chapters.

Here are some additional videos to help understand these values.

Vodie Baucham, *Manhood* and *Womanhood*:

Manhood
www.livingthatmattersbook.com/12.html

Womanhood
www.livingthatmattersbook.com/13.html

Love and Respect
www.livingthatmattersbook.com/14.html

The next link is for long-term, detailed study of biblical manhood and womanhood. Go to this site and download the PDFs, and then explore the rest of the site. It has numerous articles and forums that will be helpful. The site also does reviews on related books and other resources on this topic.

Biblical manhood/womanhood
www.livingthatmattersbook.com/15.html

Top Three Relational Values

1. *It's not about us. It's about God.*

2. *The roles of husband, as played by man, and wife, as played by woman, reflect God through authority and submission.*

3. *God sees you as one. Divorce is not part of His design.*

www.relationshipthatmatters.com

Chapter 3 to be continued ...

CHAPTER 4

Parental Values

God's Design for Parenting

As with all of the other value categories, this is not a how-to on parenting. There will be some how-to teaching in order to illustrate the values, but that is not the focus here.

Much has been written about parenting in both the Christian world and the secular world. The vast majority of it focuses on behavior, and most of it is reactive, i.e., "How do I deal with my strong-willed child?" or "How do I keep my child from drugs?"

Now if your goal is simply to control behavior, then some of this teaching can help. The truth is that all behavior can be controlled if you just "get a bigger stick." Of course I don't mean that literally—I am making a point of illustration that any behavior can be controlled with enough force.

The problem is that controlling behavior in a child does not ensure that the control will continue in an adult. Think about this. Most of us were raised with certain standards of behavior, from what time to go to bed to what to eat to our choice of friends. For many of us, those behaviors changed, either subtly or dramatically, as soon as we were away from our parents. As we got older and experienced the natural consequences of our behaviors, we slowly modified them to avoid those consequences. Or we tried to just stay a step ahead of the consequences. For some, that process can be very costly.

In addition, a great deal of the expectations of behavior placed on children by parents is purely out of preference rather than conviction. Preferences can change even from one day to the next. It may depend on the mood or circumstances. In some cases this might be okay, were it not for the fact that we present our preferences to our children like convictions, but then our behavior betrays that these are really preferences.

What this teaches children is there are no absolutes; everything is negotiable. This is exactly how they will view their responsibility in society as adults. According to many studies, not only do a majority of college students cheat regularly, they believe there is nothing wrong with it. I will share the antidote for this later, after we examine some of the values.

I am not saying that behavior is not important, but I believe the reason we focus so much attention on behavior is because of a basic lack of understanding of the purpose and goal of parenting. My prayer is that the values expressed in this chapter can help put us back on track. Although behavior is not the goal, I believe that these values will result in right behavior as well.

As with most of the values in this book, my biggest difficulty here is helping us to unlearn so many wrong things we already think we know about parenting. Someone once said, "It is better not to know so much than to know so many things which are not true." Many of the parental values that are held today have not been around that long historically, but there is a perception that things have always been this way.

When children are young, they get sick a lot, but they are very resilient. Each time they get sick, it strengthens their immune systems. Sickness actually trains the immune system to fight when one is older. Unfortunately we have been short-circuiting that process. Studies show that our overuse of antibiotics and other drugs has produced super viruses and weakened our immune systems.

Don't get me wrong. I am grateful for the many breakthroughs that have happened in children's health care. The infant mortality rate has dropped dramatically over the past fifty years. But along with those advances have come some losses.

The home used to be the center of health care. Families passed down health remedies from generation to generation. Just being sick was not a reason to visit the doctor. Most things could be treated at home. Proper nutrition came naturally; we just followed what God's Word said until science came along and told us it could do things better (homogenized milk, bovine growth hormones, corn-fed beef, etc.).

Again, I am not suggesting that we should not take full advantage of modern medicine and science. But I have seen much anxiety and stress in mothers today over the issue of health care. The slightest symptom and they are on Google.

Soon they're thinking every horrible thing is wrong with their children.

Have you heard that large quantities of researchers cause cancer in mice? Often these studies get modified until researchers get the result they want. In other words, what was bad for you yesterday is now good for you, and what was good for you yesterday now causes cancer. I am only suggesting balance here.

I want to recommend two books. The first is called *None of These Diseases* by S. I. McMillen and David E. Stern. The second is called *The Maker's Diet* by Jordan Rubin.

I believe we have done similar damage in other areas of the development of our children. We want them to have a "better life" than we have had. We do not want them to suffer in any way or do without. We make things easy for them.

We are hyperprotective of our children. When is the last time you saw children playing outside by themselves? I understand the desire to warn our children about the dangers of life, but we are making them afraid of life. As a child of the 1950s, when I speak to young parents today about this and tell them how life was for me growing up, they mostly all say the same thing: "Well, life was much safer for children back then." This is a myth.

I believe that the problem is that our reaction to this myth is doing more damage to our children than the real dangers are. Let me say that I do sympathize with this thinking. Even if you agree with me, who wants to be the one to experiment with his or her kids and end up proving me wrong?

There have been numerous studies comparing youth mortality rates in the 1950s to present times. They look at causes of death ranging from diseases to accidents to suicides and homicides. In almost every category, the mortality rate has gone down. The only increases are among homicides and suicides. I do not believe this is because children are less safe but, at least in part, because of what we are doing to them by our overprotective parental style.

Anxiety and depression are rampant among school-age children today. The amount of psychobabble flooding the Internet in an attempt to explain this is unbelievable. Children are afraid of things that they should not even know exist. They are not afraid because they are less safe. They are afraid because they feel less safe.

Mortality rate studies do not show things like molestation and kidnapping. Those things are not happening any less or more today than in the fifties. However, we hear about them instantly and constantly because of the media. And now, as back then, these things are committed by mostly by family members or family friends. Unfortunately our overprotection does not really stop that.

I know the things I have said can be taken the wrong way and can be very controversial. I am willing to risk that to make a point. I am certainly not saying we should not protect our children from danger or that we should deprive them of the best health care available. What I am saying is that the reason we overreact to these issues is because we do not understand God's basic design for parenting.

Pastor Rick Warren often says, "God cares more about your character than He does your comfort." I agree, and I think

God provides a good parental model to follow. We should be more interested in our children's characters than their comfort.

What I am asking you to do before you read on is to check your current beliefs about parenting at the door and read with an open mind. Don't worry; they will still be there when you get done. If you think I am biblically wrong, you can continue parenting as usual.

I offer this one last appeal: one study has shown that as many as 88 percent of children of evangelical families will not be following Christ by the end of their first year of college. It would be difficult to argue that the way we are parenting now is really working. (See documentation of studies at parentingthatmatters.org)

Parental Value 1
It's Not About Us; It's About Them.
It's Not About Them; It's About God

It is no surprise that most people understand and agree with the first half of this value. From the moment your child is conceived, your life is changed forever. Your rights and needs are now sacrificed for the rights and needs of that child. One of the principles stated in the relational values applies here as well. You have 100 percent authority over your children because you have 100 percent responsibility for them.

The problem is that we ignore that last half. In our culture, we have made it all about the kids. Everything in our culture is focused on the rights of kids while giving them no sense of responsibility or understanding of authority. For example, a great deal of advertising, even for adult products, is directed toward children. Children learn to want everything and to want it now.

Instead of children aspiring to become adults, we live in a culture that idolizes youth. Grown men and women behave like children living in adult bodies. I believe that this is a result of two movements that have had terrible effects on our society.

The first one is the concept of *adolescence*. The idea of adolescence did not exist until a little over a hundred years ago. Prior to that, throughout history, in most cultures you were a child until, at a culturally defined point, you went through a rite of passage and became an adult. There was no in-between stage. Adulthood happened in many cultures as young as twelve years old. This is difficult for us to imagine because few of us know any twelve-year-olds who could function as adults. This is because they were not raised and trained to become adults at age twelve—or, more accurately, they were not trained to become adults at any age.

In modern times, instead of a rite of passage, some cultures have come to rely on five measure points or milestones to determine adulthood: completing university, leaving home, getting married, having a child, and establishing financial independence. This framework presents a difficult dilemma for psychologists who promote the concept of adolescence, because young people are reaching these milestones later in life or sometimes not at all.

In Western culture, the gap between childhood and adulthood has been steadily widening over the last fifty years. Some studies show that between 50 and 80 percent of college graduates move back home with their parents. The average age of marriage is now between twenty-five and thirty and increasing every year. A growing number of young people are signing marriage contracts agreeing not to have children. Finally, fewer people are even getting married each year.

Now, the psychology gurus have added yet another stage of development. Some call it "emerging adulthood"; others call it "adultolescence." They use these terms to define what has become this long journey from adolescence to adulthood. But the sad truth is that many young people find that even after reaching some or all of the five milestones, they cannot cope with adult life. Psychologists call this a *quarter-life crisis* or QLC. After spending so many years in a lifestyle that has little resemblance to adult life, and with no training to actually live as an adult, it becomes nearly impossible for some young people to adjust. In truth, many of the things in life that should prepare people for adulthood not only do not accomplish that, but hinder it.

The second movement that radically changed how we parent was the "self-esteem" movement. As the field of child psychology developed, its practitioners emerged as self-proclaimed experts about child development. It is worth noting here that historically, before this time, we do not find widespread rebellion in children as a group. Families knew how to deal with the normal rebellious nature of their children because they understood what they were raising them to become.

The "expert" psychologists reacted to what they saw as wrong ways that children were viewed in our culture. This was rooted in some truth. Families had been moving away from God's design for parenting. We no longer understood the generational view of parenting, passing down values generation to generation. Fathers were less and less involved in the training of children.

Below is an excerpt from an article by Reb Bradley that reveals the predecessor of the self-esteem movement, a book by Dr. Spock:

> In 1946, Dr. Benjamin Spock first published his infamous book "Common Sense Book of Baby and Child Care," which was unlike any that came before it. Instead of stressing the importance of teaching self-denial and respect for authority, Spock discouraged directive training and emphasized accommodating children's feelings and catering to their preferences. No longer did children learn they could endure Brussels sprouts and suffer through daily chores. Using Spock's approach, parents began to feed self-indulgence instead of instilling self-control- homes were becoming child-centered. As parents elevated children's "freedom of expression" and natural cravings, children became more outspoken, defiant and demanding of gratification. In fact, they came to view gratification as a right.
>
> Spock wrote his book in response to a cold, authoritarian philosophy of parenting that had been dominant in America. For years, parents had been told to withhold affection from their children – not to touch them too often – not to

respond to their tears. Understanding of children had not been encouraged, and fathers had held a minor role in their nurture and care. These things distressed Spock, and they would have upset me had I been born back then. Children need our tender affection, understanding and respect. However, Spock's solutions reflected total ignorance of the hedonistic bent of human nature and fostered an over-exalted sense of self-importance in children. Homes became hotbeds for narcissism, entitlement and victim thinking.

By the 1960s, youth were rebelling en masse, not only against their own parents but against all forms of authority and structure in society—what they called "the establishment."

When these youth had grown up and had children of their own, the whole nature of parenting had changed. These parents took Dr. Spock's philosophy to a new level. Many psychologists and government leaders came to the belief that every major issue with the development of children was a result of low self-esteem.

In 1987, this led to the establishment of the California Task Force to Promote Self-Esteem and Personal and Social Responsibility. The task force's final report stated that "the lack of self-esteem is central to most personal and social ills plaguing our state and nation." John Vasconcellos, the California lawmaker responsible for the formation of the task force, compared the new emphasis on self-esteem with unlocking the secrets of the atom and the mysteries of outer space.

The result of this was a movement to remove from children's lives anything that might "damage their self-esteem." Some schools have either done away with grades or have made them irrelevant. Youth sports leagues have done away with scoring or any form of losing. Every child gets a trophy.

When all is said and done, we have raised a generation of self-centered, selfish people with a narcissistic entitlement mind-set. I am not saying that all young people today are like this, but it is such a prevailing trend that it does not even stand out as abnormal. Some have called this American Idol Syndrome. If you have ever watched the auditions, you will see people whose voices are like the sound of a dying animal, and yet they truly believe they are stars. Why? Because their family and friends constantly tell them how good they are. The following Scripture describes it well:

But mark this: There will be terrible times in the last days. People will be lovers of themselves, lovers of money, boastful, proud, abusive, disobedient to their parents, ungrateful, unholy, without love, unforgiving, slanderous, without self-control, brutal, not lovers of the good, treacherous, rash, conceited, lovers of pleasure rather than lovers of God—having a form of godliness but denying its power. Have nothing to do with such people.(1 Timothy 3:1–5 NIV)

The point of describing these movements is to identify the contrast between God's design for parenting and the way it is actually being done in our culture. The first half of the value, "It's not about us; it's about them," is not about giving our children a wonderful childhood, building up their self-esteem. It is not even about making them well behaved. It means that as parents we recognize our responsibility to prepare them for the second half of the value: "It's not about them; it's about God."

In order to explain the value "It's not about them; it's about God," we must refer back to the relational values. The second purpose of marriage is to multiply, reflecting the glory and image of God through children. Let me translate that into the parental value. If we are to raise them to reflect the glory and image of God, how do we do that?

I believe that all human beings are designed to be married. It is in our DNA. Why? Because it is in the joining of male and female together in marriage that we fully reflect the glory and image of God. If God calls someone to be single for a special purpose in life, then He must gift them to be single. It is contrary to their design. While I believe that God, indeed, sometimes does this, I believe it is the exception and not the norm.

Many people interpret Paul's words in 1 Corinthians 7 to mean that being single should be the norm. They need to take the whole chapter in context. He encourages singleness for the purpose of being completely devoted to serving God, and he says that from his heart, not as a message from God. Young people today use singleness for the purpose of serving themselves.

If it is true, that we are all designed to be married, then it would make sense that from the time we are born until we get married, we should be preparing to be married. As I have shown earlier, parenting today focuses on preparing us for nearly everything but that. We invest incredible amounts of time and energy and money preparing our children not only to have a good career, but to achieve celebrity status.

We do little to prepare them for their two most important roles in life, that of mother and father and husband and wife. Nothing will ultimately determine their fulfillment in life more than those two roles will.

I know some very wealthy and "successful" people who are miserable in large part because their marriages are miserable. I know some very poor and "unsuccessful" people who are content and happy in large part because they have a wonderful family life. There are also content rich people and discontented poor people but the common denominator seems to be the condition of the families.

That is why the real value, or God's design, is that the true goal of parenting is to prepare our children to reflect the glory and image of God through their most important roles: mother and father and husband and wife.

Let's examine this in light of Scripture to see what kind of value God places on preparing children to marry properly. We get one of our best biblical clues on godly parenting from the book of Deuteronomy.

The background of the book of Deuteronomy is that God had led His people out of slavery and brought them to the Promised Land, where He intended to bless them. The problem was that they were afraid to go in. One of the reasons they gave for not going in has some irony because it gives us insight into what we will see in Deuteronomy about parenting. They were afraid of the giants in the Promised Land—specifically, they were afraid that the giants would eat their children (Numbers 14:3; Deuteronomy 1:39). The result was that God sent them to wander in the wilderness for forty years, where they learned they could trust God.

In Deuteronomy we find that God is giving them a new opportunity to enter the Promised Land. He recounts what they have learned in the wilderness and especially His covenant with them, culminating with the retelling of the Ten Commandments in chapter 5. In chapters 6 and 7 we see this parental value come to light.

"Now this is the commandment, the statutes and the judgments which the Lord your God has commanded me to teach you, that you might do them in the land where you are going over to possess it." (Deuteronomy 6:1 NASB)

In verses 2 and 3 we see why all these commandments are important, and we will begin to understand how they relate to parenting. God's covenant is a generational covenant. It shows us how much God loves multiplication through procreation.

"Now this is the commandment, the statutes and the judgments which the LORD your God has commanded me to teach you, that you might do them in the land where you are going over to possess it, so that you and your son and your grandson might fear the Lord your God, to keep all His statutes and His commandments which I commanded you, all the days of your life, and that your days may be prolonged. O Israel, you should listen and be careful to do it, that it may be well with you and that you may multiply greatly, just as the Lord, the God of your fathers, has promised you in a land flowing with milk and honey." (Deuteronomy 6:1–3 NASB)

Up until now, we might have been tempted as parents to think this is all Old Testament and doesn't really relate to us. This is about passing on the law, i.e., the Ten Commandments, to the Israelite children, and after all we are no longer under the law. Didn't Jesus give us a new emphasis when He was asked, "What is the greatest commandment?" Isn't this what we should now be teaching our children instead of the law?

"Teacher, which is the great commandment in the law?" And He said to him, "You shall love the Lord your God with all your heart, and with all your soul, and with all your mind." "This is the great and foremost commandment." "The second is like it, You shall love your neighbor as yourself." (Matthew 22:37–39 NASB)

Now it gets real, back to Deuteronomy. Verses 4 and 5 bring it all into focus.

"Hear, O Israel! The Lord our God, The Lord is One! "You shall love the Lord your God with all your heart and with all your soul and with all your might." (Deuteronomy 6:4–5 NASB)

So Jesus was not stating something new. He was actually quoting Deuteronomy. This was always God's design. Look in Matthew again at verse 40.

"On these two commandments depend the whole law and the prophets." (Matthew 22:40 NASB)

This was always His design for us. His laws simply articulate His design. His laws teach us how to follow His design. If you want to live out the first great commandment Jesus gave, then follow the first five commandments. If you want to live out the second great commandment, then follow the last five commandments.

A good illustration of this is the movie *Karate Kid*. In the movie, a teenage boy, Daniel, is being bullied. He asks an old Okinawan man, Mr. Miyagi, to teach him karate so he can defend himself. Mr. Miyagi becomes Daniel's teacher and, slowly, a surrogate father figure.

Mr. Miyagi begins Daniel's training by having him perform menial tasks such as waxing cars, sanding a wooden floor, and painting a fence at Mr. Miyagi's house. Each chore is accomplished with specific movements involving clockwise, counterclockwise, and up-and-down hand motions. Daniel fails to see any connection between his training and these chores and eventually feels frustrated, believing he has learned nothing of karate.

When he expresses his frustration, Mr. Miyagi shows how, while doing these chores, Daniel has been learning defensive blocks through muscle memory. I refer to this as the "wax on wax off" principle.

Wax on 1
www.livingthatmattersbook.com/16.html

Wax on 2
www.livingthatmattersbook.com/17.html

Now we can see the proper view and place of behavior, and now we see the importance of behavior. Behavior is not the goal but rather the teacher. God's law teaches us His design. It brings us to Jesus. So that there is no misunderstanding about what place I am giving to the law here, I suggest that you read and study the book of Galatians.

With this view of God's law in mind, Deuteronomy next tells us how we are to instill this view in our children.

These words, which I am commanding you today, shall be on your heart. You shall teach them diligently to your sons and shall talk of them when you sit in your house and when you walk by the way and when you lie down and when you rise up. You shall bind them as a sign on your hand and they shall be as frontals on your forehead. You shall write them on the doorposts of your house and on your gates. (Deuteronomy 6:6–9 NASB)

Our children must witness in us that God is the center and passion of our lives. They must see our passion for God and His commandments in every area of our lives. When they see this, there will come a time when they will ask why we are so passionate about God and His Word.

"When your son asks you in time to come, saying, 'What do the testimonies and the statutes and the judgments mean which the Lord our God commanded you?' then you shall say to your son, 'We were slaves to Pharaoh in Egypt, and the Lord brought us from Egypt with a mighty hand. Moreover, the Lord showed great and distressing signs and wonders before our eyes against Egypt, Pharaoh and all his household; He brought us out from there in order to bring us in, to give us the land which He had sworn to our fathers.' So the Lord commanded us to observe all these statutes, to fear the Lord our God for our good always and for our survival, as it is today. It will be righteousness for us if we are careful to observe all this commandment before the Lord our God, just as He commanded us." (Deuteronomy 6:20–25 NASB)

When they ask, we are to tell them our story, how we came to trust God and follow His Word.

When my children were little, at bedtime I used to tell them what I called "Daddy stories." In essence I told them the story of my life. I would tell them how, when I was ten, my grandfather, Chet Smith, used to take me camping in the mountains. He was a miner and was knowledgeable in both geology and the Bible. He was an expert on God's creation.

Sometimes we would be walking through the mountains, and he would stop and squat down. This was my cue that I was about to get a lesson. He would pick up a plain-looking rock and explain to me the science of how God created it. Then he would hit it with his hammer and break it open, and inside there would be a beautiful crystal. I would gasp and say, "Grandpa, how did you know that was in there"? He would tell me how, when you understand God and His creation, you learn to spot the signs of how to find the beauty on the inside of God's creation that most people miss.

Then I would tell them about my other grandfather, Lee Lewis. He was a circuit preacher in Arkansas for over sixty years. He was pastor to many tiny churches all over the state who could not afford a full-time pastor. He would walk for miles from church to church. Sometimes it would take him days to get to a church. Whatever day he would arrive, that would be their Sunday, and they would have a service. When he died, the state of Arkansas issued a declaration honoring his life of service to the state.

It is important for our children to know our journey to faith. They need to know their heritage. This does not have to be about biology. My adopted children hear the same stories. In the Bible, there are two genealogies of Jesus. One is the lineage through Mary, his biological mother, and the other is through Joseph, who was not his biological father. Joseph's heritage still matters. All of us are "children of Abraham, Isaac and Jacob." The heritage of the Bible is also their heritage. I will talk more about all of this education later in the chapter.

In Deuteronomy 7, we find what all of the parental investment leads us to. It is very important to see how seriously God takes this parental value.

"When the Lord your God brings you into the land where you are entering to possess it, and clears away many nations before you, the Hittites and the Girgashites and the Amorites and the Canaanites and the Perizzites and the Hivites and the Jebusites, seven nations greater and stronger than you, and when the Lord your God delivers them before you and you defeat them, then you

*shall utterly destroy them. You shall make no covenant
with them and show no favor to them. Furthermore, you
shall not intermarry with them; you shall not give your
daughters to their sons, nor shall you take their daughters
for your sons. For they will turn your sons away from
following Me to serve other gods; then the anger of the
Lord will be kindled against you and He will quickly
destroy you."(Deuteronomy 7:1–4 NASB)*

The key is found in verses 3 and 4. We cannot allow our
children to marry outside the faith and then raise children
in a culture that is contrary to everything we just talked
about. If we do, and our descendants stop following God,
the message is that God will destroy them.

Indeed, this is what ultimately happened. The Israelites did
not follow this instruction. Their descendants did follow
other gods and were completely immersed in the idolatry of
foreign cultures. Though God was patient, He ultimately
brought judgment, and they were destroyed.

The message for us is clear. It is vital that we raise our children
to marry properly and multiply the faith.

Parental Value 2
A Mother and a Father Is a Parent

In order to fully prepare children for the life that God has
designed for them, it takes both a mother and a father. The
essence of the parental role comes from the relationship
of husband and wife. Children will come to know and

understand the nature of God and how to relate to Him from the way their mothers and fathers relate to each other. Believe it or not, your children are far more affected by the way you relate to your spouse than they are by how you relate to them.

I have illustrated this to people many times through a simple experiment. I spend about twenty minutes questioning people about their view of God. Often these are people whom I am not familiar with. I know little or nothing about their backgrounds. I ask questions about how they think God would respond to certain situations or how they think God feels about them or how they feel about God.

Then I describe back to them their parents and how the parents related to each other. Sometimes I can offer surprising details and can even tell them if their parents are still together or not—information they have not shared with me.

I am not a prophet. I do not have some special gift that I can see into their lives. It is a skill that I developed based on the fact that we form our view of God and how we relate to Him from our view of our parents and the way they relate to each other. I am talking about our practical or actual view of God, not our theological beliefs. We might answer theological questions about God differently. The questions I ask are designed to reveal personal perceptions about God that govern our behavior.

Of course, whenever I share this value, the first question I always get is, "What about single parents? Are you saying they cannot be good parents?"

Of course I am not saying that, but first let's put the question in the context of God's design. It is like saying that human beings are designed with two legs so they can walk around, and then asking, "What about people born without legs or who lose a leg in an accident? Do they not get to walk?" Modern technology has made it possible for people without legs not only to walk, but sometimes even to excel in locomotion. But that does not change the fact that the normal design is to have your own two legs. Would it not be silly and sad if we chose not to teach a child how to walk on his legs because it might make a person without legs feel bad?

In Matthew 19, Jesus had to respond to the question of divorce because it was a hot topic among differing factions of the Jews. I believe His response should also be the answer to the question we face here.

They said to Him, "Why then did Moses command to give her a certificate of divorce and send her away?" He said to them, "Because of your hardness of heart Moses permitted you to divorce your wives; but from the beginning it has not been this way." (Matthew 19:7–8 NASB)

Divorce was the result of a broken, fallen world. Jesus made it clear that this was not the way He originally designed it.

God's design is for children to be raised by a father and a mother. But God always has a backup plan because of the "hardness of our hearts." For the Israelites, this design for parenting and multiplication in building God's family was taken so seriously that He gave them some detailed backup designs for the loss of a parent. They would seem quite bizarre to our thinking today, and I do not have time to closely examine those laws. So let me just briefly show the New Testament instructions for this situation.

Religion that God our Father accepts as pure and faultless is this: to look after orphans and widows in their distress and to keep oneself from being polluted by the world. (James 1:27 NIV)

The church is to supply everything that is lacking from a missing father. I could write an entire book just on this concept and how needed it is. Frankly, the church is doing a poor job of this. I do not want to get too far off track from the main point about design, so for now I want to recommend a book to help you understand this need. It is called *Fatherless America* by David Blankenhorn.

Let me make a strong point that single parents can do an awesome job of raising their children as long as they remember that the goals are the same as those of a two-parent home. They need to take full advantage of God's provisions that compensate, as much as is possible, for the missing parent. But for now, let me show how the roles of father and mother prepare us for God's design.

In the introduction to this book, speaking about conflict, I talked about the benefits of stereoscopic vision. Each of our eyes sees from a slightly different viewpoint, and when our brain puts the two images together, we get the most accurate view. This concept is also true of parenting. Mothers and fathers each bring slightly different viewpoints that, when put together, give the best parental view. If parents are not experiencing healthy parental conflict, it means someone is not expressing his or her view.

We have all seen it: a mother telling her young son to come down from the tree before he breaks his neck, and the father encouraging him to go higher. I understand that in the application of this design, there needs to be balance and wisdom, but the design of differing views is important. Men have been uniquely designed to fill the role of father, and women have been uniquely designed to fill the role of mother.

So why are men always telling women how to be mothers and women always telling men how to be fathers? We need to trust each other to fill our respective roles, even when we do not understand it.

There is not a single verse in the Bible that, by itself, tells us specifically what the primary role of a father or a mother is. I do believe, however, that definitions can be gleaned from the totality of Scripture concerning husbands and wives and mothers and fathers.

The Role of Father

I believe that the primary role of a father is to model for his children God's unconditional love for them and how God views them. As I have already stated, this will be revealed first and foremost in the way he, as husband, relates to his wife. It is also revealed in the way he, as father, relates to his children. The Bible tells him to love his wife like Christ loved the church. This will show his children what it looks like for Christ to love the church in a visible, tangible way.

The main thing to remember is that we, as fathers, are representing God to our children. God is a great father to emulate. In the relational values, I talked about the story of

Hosea. In his relationship with his wife, he illustrated how God loved Israel. It is a great story of love.

One part of the story that is rarely brought out is the place his children had in this illustration of God's relationship with Israel. His children were given names that represented different aspects of the way God related to Israel. By now you should be familiar with a running theme in this book that every aspect of our lives is about reflecting the glory and image of God. Once again we see that being a father is "not about you; it's about them. It's not about them; it's about God."

If children do not see unconditional love and protection in their father, they may never believe they can receive those things from God. If they do not learn to trust their father, it will be difficult for them to trust God.

We can look once again at Deuteronomy to see how God modeled this for us. When the Israelites refused to go into the Promised Land, God disciplined them in order to teach them to trust Him.

"You shall remember all the way which the LORD your God has led you in the wilderness these forty years, that He might humble you, testing you, to know what was in your heart, whether you would keep His commandments or not. "He humbled you and let you be hungry, and fed you with manna which you did not know, nor did your fathers know, that He might make you understand that man does not live by bread alone, but man lives by everything that proceeds out of the mouth of the LORD. "Your clothing did not wear out on you, nor did your foot swell these forty years. "Thus you are to know in your

heart that the LORD your God was disciplining you just as a man disciplines his son. (Deuteronomy 8:2–5 NASB).

At its core this basically involves teaching your children all of the values in this book—not because they are in this book, but because they come from *the* book, the Word of God. In relationship to this primary role, it begins with teaching them to trust and obey you, and through that to trust and obey God.

The Role of Mother

I believe that the primary role of the mother is to model how her children are to view God and how to relate to God. She does this primarily in the way she, as wife, relates to her husband, but also in the way that she, as mother, relates to her children. The Bible tells her to submit to her husband as unto the Lord, and as the church submits to Jesus. This will show her children how to submit to God and how to relate to Jesus.

Mothers in our culture can get caught up in the chores of motherhood and miss the more important role. The story of Mary and Martha illustrates this.

"Now as they were traveling along, He entered a village; and a woman named Martha welcomed Him into her home. She had a sister called Mary, who was seated at the Lord's feet, listening to His word. But Martha was distracted with all her preparations; and she came up to Him and said, "Lord, do You not care that my sister has left me to do all the serving alone? Then tell her to help

me." But the Lord answered and said to her, "Martha, Martha, you are worried and bothered about so many things; but only one thing is necessary, for Mary has chosen the good part, which shall not be taken away from her." (Luke 10:38–42 NASB)

I understand that the constant caring for the needs of children cannot be avoided, but those things do not define the role of mother. I have stated that people develop their views of how they think God views them from their fathers. But they get their desire and passion for God from their mothers. They also learn the way they will relate to all authority from the way their mothers relate to their fathers.

Staying Focused on the Goal Preparing Them to Be Husbands and Wives, Fathers and Mothers

So how do we accomplish the goal of preparing children for their most important roles in life—those of mother and father and husband and wife?

It is interesting to me that when parents become obsessed with other goals than this for their children, they seem to know instinctively what to do. Sports-minded families start their children early in the sport of choice. They spend thousands of dollars on private coaching or club teams. They subordinate everything in their schedules to the priority of driving the kids to practice, lessons, and games. They are willing to give up their own wants and needs to purchase whatever clothing and equipment are needed to make their children successful in the sport of choice. They make men and women who are successful in the sports world the heroes and idols for their children.

Entertainment or performance-minded families make similar sacrifices for their children. They start them in singing or acting lessons before they even know what those things are. I have seen parents get an agent for their children before they can walk or talk. Naturally, children enjoy these things, so it is easy for parents to say they are doing it all for their children. They make men and women who are successful in entertainment the heroes and idols for their children.

Career or education-minded families do all that is necessary to ensure that from preschool to grad school, their children get the best training possible, no matter what the cost or sacrifice. They are proud of how disciplined and hardworking their children are. They take great comfort in knowing their children will be able to take care of themselves and be successful. They make men and women with successful careers or superior intellects the heroes and idols for their children.

Even marriage-minded parents seem to know what to do. They focus on teaching their children to be as attractive as possible. This includes learning how to be popular, socially cool, and acceptable. Often, this goes hand in hand with the activities of all the above-mentioned parents and helps to legitimize their goals. Marriage-minded parents tend to highlight the traits of beautiful women or macho men. They make beautiful, popular people and famous couples the heroes and idols for their children.

How sad it is, then, that when it comes to preparing children for their most important roles and ensuring they will become adults with godly values and character, most parents seem clueless. Not all of these parents feel clueless. They convince themselves that they are actually instilling godly values because they add God and faith into the mix of all the lifestyles above. I have already shown that this is far from the truth. The facts show that the children of most Christian parents are not growing up to be healthy nor godly husbands and wives, mothers and fathers.

I want to make something very clear about the illustrations above. I am not saying those things are in and of themselves bad. Anyone who knows me knows that I love sports, performing, and education. The illustration is to show that when we are passionate about something, we will find a way to instill that passion in our children. Let's make that passion be about God.

Many young girls, five and six years old, are experts at everything "princess." They know all the princess characters' names and what they wear. These girls want to wear the same dresses and hear the stories.

Likewise, many young boys are experts on all things "cars." They know who Mater is. They can tell you the make and model of all of their Matchbook cars.

For other children, the focus might be pirates or music or Elmo or Veggie Tales. So how do these children become experts, obsessed with things at such an early age? They did not just suddenly one day ask their parents. They were saturated with these concepts from the time they could recognize them. They saw the joy and excitement in their parents as they filled their lives with these things.

I am not saying that children do not sometimes show a natural interest on their own initiative. What I am saying is that without parental stimulation and saturation, that interest does not usually last.

Let's look back at Deuteronomy again. Remember that God is instructing them about the things that are to be passed down, remembered, and valued from generation to generation.

Impress them on your children. Talk about them when you sit at home and when you walk along the road, when you lie down and when you get up. Tie them as symbols on your hands and bind them on your foreheads. Write them on the doorframes of your houses and on your gates. (Deuteronomy 6:7–9 NIV)

This principle of passionate saturation works because it is how God designed children to learn. They must be exposed to these values from the time they are conceived. I tell fathers all the time: from the day you find out your wife is pregnant, begin reading a chapter of Proverbs out loud to the womb every day. Let it become a habit before the baby is even born. Let their heroes become the men and women of Hebrews 11, God's faith hall of fame. Let them see excitement in your eyes every time you talk about the Bible or God.

It would be wonderful if little girls were as well versed at what a virtuous woman is as they are about princesses. It would be wonderful if little boys knew as much about David's mighty men as they do about Iron Man. But most of all, it would be wonderful if little boys and girls believed that the Bible is their family's most prized possession, a book passionately loved by their mother and father.

This is important because the Bible is the number one tool we have for teaching our children. Most children do not know if their parents ever read or study the Bible. They need to see that before they even understand what the Bible is.

From childhood you have known the sacred writings which are able to give you the wisdom that leads to salvation through faith which is in Christ Jesus. All Scripture is inspired by God and profitable for teaching, for reproof, for correction, for training in righteousness; so that the man of God may be adequate, equipped for every good work. (2 Timothy 3:15–17 NASB)

The Process
The Big Picture View

When we use stereoscopic vision to put the role of father and the role of mother together and look at the big picture, we can better understand the process. The process of preparing children for their roles in marriage looks like this; they will go from:

Healthy Dependence, Obedience, and Trust
↓
Healthy Independence and Self-Discipline
↓
Healthy Interdependence and Reproduction

The average family operates in one of two extremes, both of which corrupt this process. Both extremes have the same result: preventing them from reaching the healthy interdependence necessary for relationship. (The Vows for Husbands and Wives in the relational values chapter illustrate healthy interdependence.)

However, in the Lord, neither is woman independent of man, nor is man independent of woman. For as the woman originates from the man, so also the man has his birth *through the woman; and all things originate from God. (1 Corinthians 11:11–12 NASB)*

Some families operate on a model of extreme strictness, either for the purpose of controlling behavior or as a result of being overprotective. This is not healthy dependence, and children in such environments don't learn healthy independence. They do not develop self-discipline. They are likely to rebel in an unhealthy way. If you do not give children safe ways to develop independence, they will find unsafe ways. For example, if at the proper age a child is not given an opportunity to experiment with something like hairstyle and fail, he might later experiment with something like drugs and fail.

Some families operate on a model of permissive or indulgent parenting. They want to give their children total freedom so as not to crush their creative spirits. There are few or no rules in such households. Parents are more concerned with children's comfort than their characters. This brings the same result as overly strict parenting. Children cannot find healthy independence because they never experienced healthy dependence and learned self-discipline.

Following God's design for the primary roles of fathers and mothers, as I said earlier, is the only way to properly go through the three stages of preparing children for marriage and parenthood. When a child is younger, in the healthy dependence stage, he must learn from his father complete and unquestioned obedience, which comes from complete and total trust. Ultimately the father teaches his child to trust God. He does this by modeling the unconditional love and faithfulness of God. I have already shown that this is the parenting model of God. As He took His people from infancy to maturity, He began with the need for obedience in order to teach them that they could trust Him.

In the healthy dependence stage, the mother also plays a vital role in teaching obedience and trust. She teaches her children that the fear of the Lord is the beginning of wisdom. This is not a bad fear. This is the fear of obedience and trust. She will also model for them and inspire in them a passion to love and please God. The best way to do this is to model this through her passion for and submission to her husband.

I have just summarized for you the first five chapters of Proverbs. It describes how you begin with trust and obedience and then move to discernment and wisdom, which will give the right perspective on relationships.

Give prudence to the naïve, to the youth knowledge and discretion. (Proverbs 1:4 NASB)

The fear of the Lord is the beginning of wisdom; Fools despise wisdom and instruction. Hear, my son, your father's instruction and do not forsake your mother's teaching. (Proverbs 1:7–8 NASB)

Let your fountain be blessed,
And rejoice in the wife of your youth. (Proverbs 5:18)

Moving from healthy dependence to healthy independence to healthy interdependence is the big picture view. We cannot lose sight of this as we narrow our focus.

Parental Value 3
Godly Parenting Is About Discipline, Resulting in Godliness, Not About Punishment, Controlling Behavior

Godliness is the reverent awareness of God's sovereignty over every aspect of life, and the attendant determination to honor Him in all one's conduct.

It sometimes may seem like there is a fine line between discipline and punishment. Some may think it is just a matter of semantics, and discipline and punishment are the same. In truth they are very different. Punishment is payback or retribution or a penalty for a past action. It is used to satisfy the debt incurred by that action. Discipline is training for future actions that are in harmony with God's design.

To fully grasp this value or design, revisit a principle I shared in the introduction of the book. I must *respond* to my children according to what I know rather than *react* to what I feel. This is a key difference between punishment and discipline.

Punishment is usually a reaction to how the child's action makes the parent feel. Discipline is a response to what the parents knows about God's design. Discipline is used to bring the child into harmony with God's design. The ultimate desire of parental discipline is to bring children to a place of self-discipline.

Punishment is a penalty for wrong behavior, in the hope of instilling right behavior. The right behavior itself is the goal. Discipline has as its goal the use of behavior to develop godly character. In this case, right behavior is a tool, but godly character is the goal.

There are many parents who, through the use of effective punishment, control behavior in their children. On the exterior, this looks great. People compliment these parents on how well behaved their kids are. Often, when those children become adults, there is no self-control. They choose destructive behaviors without the moral compass of character to protect them. What is even worse is that some of them will continue the behaviors out of sheer habit, but they are empty inside and do not know how to cope with the stress and pain of life.

It is important to note that the difference between punishment and discipline is not about the act. The difference is in the attitude or goal of the parent. The same act can be punishment or discipline.

For example, if a parent gets angry when a child disobeys and starts yelling at the child while spanking, this is a punishment. If the parent, in firmness but calmness, administers a promised spanking in response to the child's actions, this is discipline.

Discipline happens when the child sees the correlation between behavior and the resulting consequence. Punishment happens when the child primarily sees a correlation between the parent's anger, frustration, or disappointment and the resulting consequence.

There are three basic words that describe what discipline looks like. I encourage you to imprint these words on your brain. They will let you know if you are disciplining for the purpose of godliness.

Discipline must be:

> *Matter-of-Fact*
> *Immediate*
> *Consistent*

Matter-of-Fact

Discipline should never be done in reaction to anger or frustration. Once we express anger or frustration to our children, they focus on us as the issue rather than on their actions. They believe there would not be an issue if we were not upset. We must let them know that their actions are wrong and the results will happen whether we are upset or not.

But being matter-of-fact does not simply mean that we are without anger or frustration. It means that the discipline should be in response to facts. There must be clearly defined rules. or "laws". If you do not articulate to children the "if/then" of their behavior, then there cannot be true discipline. In Deuteronomy and throughout the Bible, God continually articulates what is proper behavior. He declares what the outcome will be if we obey and what the outcome will be if we do not.

Rules take the focus off of you. Children will always know that what is happening to them is a direct result of their actions. Even if you choose a discipline that is over the top in comparison to the violation, children will still know that it was their choice that brought that result, and that a right choice could have prevented that result.

Immediate

If we are to teach children the correlation between their actions and the results, then discipline must be immediate. Whenever I hear a parent counting to three or warning "If you do that one more time ..." I know the child is not learning this correlation. If a child clearly understands what the rule is, and you witness the child violating it, then the child has already done it "one more time." When a parent asks in frustration, "How many times do I have to tell you?" he or she has already answered the question—it is more than once. The discipline must be administered the first time and every time a child violates the rule, and it must be done immediately.

This also means that the response of discipline must be a price a child will not be willing to pay. There are some children, for example, who are willing to pay the price of a time-out to get their way. For each violation of the same law, the price needs to go up. Perhaps on the first offense the discipline might be a ten-minute time-out. If that same offense is committed several more times, it is obvious the child is willing to pay that price. The time-out should then be raised to thirty minutes or be changed to something different altogether (taking a toy away, etc.).

Please remember that this is not a how-to book. Therefore, I am not focusing on the specifics of the discipline but rather on the principles that govern the administration of the discipline. You must know each child well to know what the proper response (discipline) is for him or her.

Consistent

None of this will work if the discipline is not consistent. It must be applied every single time, without fail. Imagine how difficult life would be if things like gravity only worked half of the time, at random. We would never really be able to comply. God's design works every single time, and the consequences of ignoring that design teach us to be in harmony with His design.

The key to consistent discipline lies in understanding the difference between conviction and preference. The biggest difference is that preference implies choice and it can change. There used to be a popular bumper sticker and slogan that said, "God said it, I believe it, and that settles it!" That is wrong. It should say, "God said it and that settles it, whether I believe it or not!"

Often when I talk with people about the values in this book, their lives are not in harmony with the values. They get uncomfortable and want to explain to me why their circumstances are different. They say things like, "Okay, that is true, but …"

I immediately interrupt them and say, "Stop! Truth never has a but …" Preferences can have a "but …" Truth never changes.

We tend to think that something is a conviction if we believe it strongly enough. Believe it or not, the US Supreme Court has actually ruled on this issue of the difference between preference and conviction. They said a preference can be a belief that is so strongly held that a person will give all of his wealth to support it. However, they said, a preference is nevertheless a belief that one will change under certain circumstances. The court further ruled that for something to be considered a conviction, a man must believe that his God requires it of him and therefore circumstances cannot change it.

Our belief in something does not determine whether it is true or not. Belief only changes how we relate to that truth. All truth is true, but not all truth has the same value to us. For example, if someone were to put a gun to my head and tell me that if I do not say that Abraham Lincoln was not the sixteenth president of the United States, he will blow my brains out, I would say, "Who is Abraham Lincoln?" But if he told me I had to say Jesus Christ is not God, I would say, "Then just pull the trigger." Both of those facts are true, but they do not have the same value to me.

Conviction is a belief in a truth that can never change regardless of circumstances. These beliefs are nonnegotiable. If it is true today, it will be true tomorrow. I am not saying that you should be willing to die for every conviction you have, but you certainly should be willing to live for them.

So what does this have to do with consistency in discipline? We present many of our rules or laws to our children as if these are convictions, but then we live as if they are preferences. We are inconsistent in what we say as opposed to what we do. This has the effect of making our children believe everything is negotiable. They do not value your rules or fear the results of violating them because they are not convinced that these really are the rules.

When I was a child, my family was not what I would consider poor, but we certainly did not have excess. At Christmastime we always knew that we would get one present. We could make three choices from out of the Sears catalog and hope to get one of those.

This had two results on my behavior. First, for several months out of the year, the Sears catalog was my friend. Since I was to get only one thing all year, I had to make a good choice. The second effect was that when I did get that present, I cherished it deeply. I took good care of it. I was never bored with it. It had great value to me.

Contrast that with kids today. I see this even in relatively poor families. They get many presents from many sources. Before they even finish unwrapping one present, their minds are on the next one. There are so many stimuli in their lives that nothing retains its value for long. They get bored easily.

This is the same thing that happens when we have too many rules that are based on preferences. None of them have any real value. I am not saying that you cannot have any rules based on preference. But we must not treat them the same way as the rules based on conviction. We need to clearly articulate to our children the laws that are nonnegotiable and will never change.

They must learn to depend on the fact that the consequences for violating those rules will happen every time.

How?

I said in the beginning that this is not a how-to on parenting. However, I want to give you a big picture view of how to live out the parental values. I hope you have been able to grasp the essence of what I believe is God's design for parenting. The goal is to prepare (train) our children for their greatest roles: those of mother and father, husband and wife. Then, through those roles, they can fully reflect the glory and image of God. Preparation is done by a mother and father, who model for the children how God relates to us and how we relate to God.

I have demonstrated how far off we are from this design. As a result, parenting in our culture seems complicated and overwhelming. That is a shame, because it is really quite simple.

Let me share with you my simple plan for how to accomplish this. I hope it should go without saying that children need to know the fifteen values stated in this book, but in addition there are three other things:

1. Make your children experts in the fifteen values expressed in this book and the Vows of Husbands and Wives from chapter 3.
2. Make your children experts at Psalms and Proverbs. Read one chapter of Proverbs and five chapters of Psalms every day.

3. Make your children experts at basic theology. Catechism is the best way to do this. Below are some really good ones.

Reformed reader
www.livingthatmattersbook.com/18.html

Desiring God
www.livingthatmattersbook.com/19.html

Teaching tools
www.livingthatmattersbook.com/20.html

That's it! I believe that if you personally live the relational designs of chapter 3 and then passionately saturate your children with these three things, your children will grow up to be godly husbands and wives, mothers and fathers. These three things must be more important than academic training, more important than social training, more important than physical training. All of those things should happen, but in the context of these three things.

Making children experts at the vows means, in essence, preparing them for the roles of husband and wife. If they are experts at the vows, they will be experts at the roles.

Making them experts in Proverbs and Psalms is, in essence, teaching them how to rightly relate to God and how to rightly relate to life. Proverbs is important because it teaches us wisdom. Wisdom is seeing the world through God's eyes. Proverbs was written by the wisest man who ever lived. In the first few chapters, he tells his sons that if they follow the wisdom of these proverbs, then they will be successful in life. Psalms is important because it teaches us how to talk to God. It shows us how to voice our discontent in the context of praise and trust. For these reasons I believe Proverbs is best, though not exclusively, taught by the father. I believe that Psalms is best, though not exclusively, taught by the mother.

Links for further study:

World view
www.livingthatmattersbook.com/21.html

Home school
www.livingthatmattersbook.com/22.html

Character tools and resources
www.livingthatmattersbook.com/23.html

The teaching from this ministry influenced me greatly when I was young. There are some people who strongly disagree with some of the teachings and approaches, but I believe the resources you will find on this site for teaching your children are unparalleled.

Top Three Parental Values

1. *It's not about us; it's about them.*
   It's not about them; it's about God.

2. *A mother and a father is a parent.*

3. *Godly parenting is about discipline, resulting in godliness, not about punishment, controlling behavior.*

www.parentingthatmatters.org

Chapter 4 to be continued ...

CHAPTER 5

Sexual Values

God's Design for Sexuality

In the previous chapter, I talked about the difference between preference and conviction. The difference is so important that the US Supreme Court gave a legal ruling on the difference. I believe that when it comes to sexual beliefs, most Christians today are guided by preference, not conviction. Many believe that biblical teachings on sexuality are culturally biased and outdated.

The result is that, for most Christians, their view of sexuality is far more in harmony with a humanist worldview than with God's design. Pornography is now mainstream and an accepted part of our culture. In fact, images that once would have been considered pornography are now on prime-time television in hamburger and lingerie commercials. Homosexuality is considered normal and natural, and those who disagree are called homophobic bigots. A majority of Americans, including many Christians, now favor same-sex marriage. Many Christian parents believe that it is inevitable their children will have sex before marriage. They just strongly encourage that it be with someone the child *really loves* in a committed relationship. They believe that the best they can do is to make sure a child has "safe sex."

Despite all of the educational programs to prevent it, teen pregnancy not only continues to be a major issue but has taken on a new twist. Great effort is being put forth to help pregnant teens. This is a good thing, but it has had an unintended side effect. Many of the consequences and much of the stigma attached to teen pregnancy are disappearing. There are some high schools that now allow girls to bring their babies to school. Even the church honors these young girls for choosing not to have abortions. Many celebrities are choosing to have babies without being married. This is inspiring young girls to get pregnant intentionally rather than treating unwed parenthood as something to be avoided.

Along with this new mainstream view of sexuality have come much darker results. Human trafficking is a worldwide epidemic. Pedophilia, incest, rape, and other forms of sexual abuse are as common in the news as the weather report. STDs are so common that instead of PSAs warning against them, we see an abundance of advertisements about how to treat them. The STDs that once brought shame are now nearly a badge of honor. Finally, abortion and its tragic effects are still on the increase. The majority of convicted serial killers admit to being addicted to pornography. It would seem that our new free-love society is not so free after all. It has come with a very high price. No civilization has ever survived after adopting these views on sexuality.

Believe it or not, there is actually a good side to all of this. It begs a very important question. Why has Satan worked so hard to corrupt our society's thinking about sexuality? It is because he understands how important sexuality is to God. For too long the church has taken the attitude that all sex is dirty. The church should be leading the way in sexual freedom, but modeling that true sexual freedom comes only in the context of God's design: the context of the marriage union between a man and a woman. Instead, many Christians have gone from what they see as a repressive, restrictive, religious view of sexuality to a secular, worldly view.

There is no greater sexual freedom than living according to God's sexual design. I hope I can effectively articulate that design for you in this chapter.

Freedom from sexual sin
www.livingthatmattersbook.com/24.html

For this is the will of God, your sanctification; that is, that you abstain from sexual immorality; that each of you know how to possess his own vessel in sanctification and honor, not in lustful passion, like the Gentiles who do not know God; and that no man transgress and defraud his brother in the matter because the Lord is the avenger in all these things, just as we also told you before and solemnly warned you. For God has not called us for the purpose of impurity, but in sanctification. So, he who rejects this is

*not rejecting man but the God who gives His Holy Spirit
to you. (1 Thessalonians4:3–8 NASB)*

If we are to win the battle against sexual immorality, the
children of God must get on the same page. Often when
Christians stand for purity, it is other Christians who make
them feel like prudes or just "not cool." These verses in
Thessalonians should stop us dead in our tracks. When we
do not help each other stand against immorality, we are
literally opposing God!

Sexual Value 1
My Body Does Not Belong to Me;
It Belongs to God. It Will Either
Reflect or Dishonor His Glory

*Therefore I urge you, brethren, by the mercies of God, to
present your bodies a living and holy sacrifice, acceptable
to God, which is your spiritual service of worship. And
do not be conformed to this world, but be transformed by
the renewing of your mind, so that you may prove what
the will of God is, that which is good and acceptable and
perfect.*

*For through the grace given to me I say to everyone among
you not to think more highly of himself than he ought to
think; but to think so as to have sound judgment, as God
has allotted to each a measure of faith. For just as we
have many members in one body and all the members do
not have the same function, so we, who are many, are one*

body in Christ, and individually members one of another. (Romans 12:1–5 NASB)

"I have the right to do anything," you say—but not everything is beneficial. "I have the right to do anything"— but I will not be mastered by anything. You say, "Food for the stomach and the stomach for food, and God will destroy them both." The body, however, is not meant for sexual immorality but for the Lord, and the Lord for the body. By his power God raised the Lord from the dead, and he will raise us also. Do you not know that your bodies are members of Christ himself? Shall I then take the members of Christ and unite them with a prostitute? Never! Do you not know that he who unites himself with a prostitute is one with her in body? For it is said, "The two will become one flesh." But whoever is united with the Lord is one with him in spirit.

Flee from sexual immorality. All other sins a person commits are outside the body, but whoever sins sexually, sins against their own body. Do you not know that your bodies are temples of the Holy Spirit, who is in you, whom you have received from God? You are not your own; you were bought at a price. Therefore honor God with your bodies. (1 Corinthians 6:12–20 NIV)

As bond slaves of Jesus Christ, we are to yield all rights over our bodies. We must completely change our way of thinking. Our bodies have been bought and paid for by the blood of Jesus. He set us free from the law of sin and death. We are now part of His body. Everything that we do in our bodies, we make Him a part of. This is a difficult concept to fully wrap our brains around, but as I said, our way of thinking must be transformed.

This new thinking must change everything about how we view our bodies. It means that we will look different, dress differently, and behave differently. This brings a special significance to our sexuality. The Bible repeats several times the phrase, "They two shall be one flesh." When you put together all of the biblical explanations and contexts of the phrase, you will see that when we are joined sexually, there is much more going on than just the joining of our bodies.

God takes sexuality very seriously. Sexuality has the potential to draw us into closer fellowship with Christ or drive wedge between Him and us.

"You have heard that it was said, 'You shall not commit adultery'; but I say to you that everyone who looks at a woman with lust for her has already committed adultery with her in his heart. If your right eye makes you stumble, tear it out and throw it from you; for it is better for you to lose one of the parts of your body, than for your whole body to be thrown into hell. If your right hand makes you stumble, cut it off and throw it from you; for it is better for you to lose one of the parts of your body, than for your whole body to go into hell. (Matthew 5:27–30 NASB)

It is easy to explain this as not having a literal meaning, but in doing so we must not miss the intensity of this message. God views the corruption of sexuality so strongly that He is telling us that we need to be willing to go to any extreme to avoid it.

Stop and meditate on that for a moment. In Christianity today, sexuality has become a way of showing the world that we are "cool," that we are not prudes. We joke about it and feel proud that no one can accuse of us of being sexually repressed.

The point of this value is that everything we do in this body will either bring glory to God or shame. This is especially true of our sexuality. It will either bring immense glory and honor to God, or it will destroy every good thing we do in Him.

Satan knows this. This is why he lies to us about sexuality. His biggest lie is, "It's no big deal." God says that it is a very big deal. Our bodies belong to Him and not to us.

At the 2004 Desiring God Conference, John Piper made two very profound statements about sexuality. He said, "The first is that sexuality is designed by God as a way to know God in Christ more fully. And the second is that, knowing God in Christ more fully, is designed as a way of guarding and guiding our sexuality."

Please watch this video before continuing. It is a powerful message helping to define this value.

Sex and the Supremacy of Christ
www.livingthatmattersbook.com/25.html

This value points us right back to the spiritual value that *we are designed for intimate fellowship with God*. Through healthy sexuality between husband and wife we can know

God more deeply, and through that intimate fellowship with God we find safety from corrupted sexuality.

God Has Delegated the Sexual Stewardship of My Body to My Spouse

Now concerning the things about which you wrote, it is good for a man not to touch a woman. But because of immoralities, each man is to have his own wife, and each woman is to have her own husband. The husband must fulfill his duty to his wife, and likewise also the wife to her husband. The wife does not have authority over her own body, but the husband does; and likewise also the husband does not have authority over his own body, but the wife does. Stop depriving one another, except by agreement for a time, so that you may devote yourselves to prayer, and come together again so that Satan will not tempt you because of your lack of self-control. (1 Corinthians 7:1–5 NASB)

I have established that God owns my body. Here we see that God has delegated sexual authority over my body to my wife and authority over my wife's body to me. In chapter 3, I also showed that the biblical view of authority is about protection. We are to mutually protect one another sexually.

The city of Corinth of that day was what we might call the pornography capital of the world. It was known for sexual perversions. The church in Corinth was being influenced by a group called Gnostics. Gnostics put supreme value on knowledge and believed humans should transcend the physical to a higher plane of existence. They taught that the only way to battle sexual immorality was to abstain from sex altogether. In fact, they said it was better just to avoid marriage. The church at Corinth wrote to Paul, asking what he thought about this, and in this passage he is responding.

His answer was that the truth is exactly the opposite of what the Gnostics were saying. The best lifestyle for protection from immorality is through regular, healthy sex between a husband and wife. (The Greek word translated as "immorality" is *porneias*, from which we get the word *pornography*.) He went on to say that it is a wife's duty to protect her husband by meeting his sexual needs, and it is the husband's duty to protect his wife by meeting her sexual needs. Withholding from your spouse is like stealing. He made it clear that to abstain from this, even for good and righteous reasons, for more than a short period of time would open the door for Satan to attack.

This is not a declaration for sex on demand. That is why God made this a mutual stewardship. If a man says to his wife, "I want sex now, and your body belongs to me," could she not just as well say, "Your body belongs to me, and I am telling you to keep it off of me"? This is about mutual serving and protecting and nurturing.

This is difficult to define, but I believe if you are living the vows from the relational values chapter, this will make more sense. Watch again the two videos linked earlier in the chapter.

Sexual Value 2
Through Sexuality a Husband and Wife Reflect the Glory and Image of God to Each Other

In the relational values chapter, I showed how the role of husband and the role of wife reflect the image of the triune God. I believe that those roles primarily reflect His image to and through the church. The roles give a picture of how the church relates to Jesus. The Bible often compares the relationship between Christ and the church to that of a husband and wife. Think of the family as the body of Christ at the cellular level. That is why Satan attacks marriage. Cancer always strikes the body at the cellular level.

In this case the sexual roles of the husband and wife reflect the glory and image of God to and through each other and, in turn, enhance the way their relational roles reflect it to and through the church. I know that sounds complicated and confusing, so let me explain how this works.

The next few paragraphs are likely to be the most controversial in the book because it is a very difficult concept to articulate and will be easily misunderstood. Please make sure you follow the links to videos and articles for further explanations.

Throughout history, the way that God has related to His people, whether individually or as a group, has always been as the pursuer. We would never seek God if He did not send His Spirit to draw us. Relationship with God is given freely by His grace and is undeserved, but intimate fellowship with Him has some conditions. Jesus said, "You are my friends if you keep my commandments."

Even so, when we are broken before Him and worship Him, He grants us that intimacy in spite of our failures. When we experience that intimacy with Him, it highly motivates us to want to please Him in every way.

The sexual roles of the husband and wife illustrate this. I believe that sometimes men get a bad rap for supposedly just wanting sex and not intimacy. But the reality is that it is in their design to move to emotional intimacy through physical intimacy. It is this design that causes them to instinctively be pursuers.

Women are designed to respond better to physical intimacy through emotional intimacy. They also get a bad rap through the "not tonight, I have a headache" stereotype. But they are designed to respond physically in the context of love and security, the way a rose opens its bloom with the right nourishment and light. Otherwise, it is just a thorn bush. Got that, men?

It may sound like the two designs are at odds. But when we celebrate each other's design instead of rejecting it, a magical thing happens. It is a paradox of design that can teach us much about how we relate to God. I do not have proof, but I believe men and women produce the hormone oxytocin differently. This hormone, among other things, causes us to bond. In the female, it happens through a process of touching and caressing. This gives her a desire for sex. In the male, it happens through sex and causes him to feel deep love for her.

By the way, Paul also had a difficult time explaining this concept:

For this reason a man shall leave his father and mother and shall be joined to his wife, and the two shall become one flesh. This mystery is great; but I am speaking with reference to Christ and the church. (Ephesians 5:31–32 NASB)

Sexual Value 3
The Male Body and the Female Body Are Designed to Become One Flesh. They Fit Together to Reflect the Glory and Image of God through Creation

For this reason a man shall leave his father and his mother, and be joined to his wife; and they shall become one flesh. And the man and his wife were both naked and were not ashamed. (Genesis 2:24–25)

God created man in His own image, in the image of God He created him; male and female He created them. God blessed them; and God said to them, "Be fruitful and multiply, and fill the earth, and subdue it; and rule over the fish of the sea and over the birds of the sky and over every living thing that moves on the earth." (Genesis 1:27–28 NASB)

I do not think I need to make much of an argument for the fact that, physically and sexually speaking, the male and female bodies are quite different. Not only are most people very aware of this fact, they are in general happy about it. Hence the popular French declaration, "Vive la différence." It means long live the difference between males and females.

What is not so readily accepted, yet is no less a fact, is the complementary and interdependent nature of this difference. Though the bodies are different, they fit together perfectly and are complementary in more ways than the obvious one of intercourse. That is why, in the Scripture passage above, although the phrase "one flesh" primarily means intercourse, it also means much more. Let's look at some of the ways male and female bodies are complementary, beginning with the obvious.

Genitalia

You may laugh and say well, duh, of course the male and female genitalia fit together in a complementary way. But you may not have thought about why and how, and how much this contrasts with the incompatibility of same-sex intercourse. I do not mean to be crude, but it is much more than simply fitting Tab A into Slot B.

The vagina is designed to be penetrated. The muscles are configured to pull in. It produces natural lubricants to making penetration easier. The texture inside the vagina is designed in a way that not only facilitates penetration, with a focus on uniting sperm and egg, but is also designed for pleasure. (The importance of sexual pleasure will come to light later in this chapter.) The vagina is also designed to withstand rigorous penetration.

The anus and rectum by contrast are definitely not designed to be penetrated. The muscles are configured to push out. It is dry and smooth. The lining is thin and easily torn, allowing for disease and infection to spread. Medical science tells us that anal intercourse is the most risky form of sexual activity.

The penis, as we know, has multiple functions. It excretes liquid body waste through the urethra. It produces sperm and other fluids necessary to protect and transport the sperm. It is designed uniquely to deposit that sperm in the vagina. (I find it amazing that the same system used to expel the liquid waste product of life is also used to deliver the liquid catalyst of life.)

The penis is perfectly designed for penetrating the vagina, and the vagina has a perfect design to stimulate it to ejaculation, depositing the sperm in a perfect way to reach the egg for fertilization and the creation of life.

There are components in male ejaculate that are immunosuppressive. In the course of ordinary reproductive physiology, this allows the sperm to evade the immune defenses of the female. In anal sex, however, it heightens the risk for spreading disease and infections.

Forgive the graphic nature of this value, but I believe it is necessary to strongly make this point. I believe that no scientist or medical doctor with integrity can avoid believing that sexuality is designed to be between a male and a female. Working in harmony together, they are the producers of life. If scientists apply the same logic and criteria to this that they do to any other fact, I believe this will be an unavoidable truth.

Therefore God gave them over in the lusts of their hearts to impurity, so that their bodies would be dishonored among them. For they exchanged the truth of God for a lie, and worshiped and served the creature rather than the Creator, who is blessed forever. Amen.

For this reason God gave them over to degrading passions; for their women exchanged the natural function for that which is unnatural, and in the same way also the men abandoned the natural function of the woman and burned in their desire toward one another, men with men committing indecent acts and receiving in their own persons the due penalty of their error. (Romans 1:24–27 NASB)

Interdependence

However, in the Lord, neither is woman independent of man, nor is man independent of woman. For as the woman originates from the man, so also the man has his birth through the woman; and all things originate from God. (1 Corinthians 11:11–12 NASB)

The design and perfect fit of male and female bodies give us a picture of the interdependent natures of male and female. The woman was created out of the man, but then new life comes through the woman.

Medical science has come really far in the reproductive field. Scientists would almost have us believe that they can create life in a test tube. They can impregnate a woman without intercourse through artificial insemination. But the plain and simple truth is that they cannot create either a human egg or human sperm. These can only come from male and female bodies. Male and female genitalia are perfectly designed to unite the sperm and the egg. The artificial way that science brings this about is expensive and often unsuccessful. God's design is so good that life is created often in spite of extreme efforts to prevent it, which is why abortion even exists.

This is important because, once again, I propose that if scientists were intellectually honest instead of politically correct, they would boldly proclaim that homosexuality is contrary to nature and the design of the universe. They would celebrate the interdependent nature of male and female bodies for the survival of the human race.

Homosexuality

I believe that anyone reading this book who is either homosexual or views homosexuality as proper is sure to view me as a homophobic bigot. This saddens me deeply. I love all people. My belief that the Bible teaches that homosexual acts are sinful and contrary to God's design is honest and sincere. I do not hate you. I do not wish you ill. I do not trust the government, through laws, to tell you what you can or cannot do, any more than I trust them to tell me what I can or cannot do. Marriage should be a spiritual covenant, not a legal contract. But just because I passionately share my belief with you does not mean that I hate you or that I am controlling your life.

I have, throughout my life, had many friends who were self-proclaimed gays or lesbians. I have relatives who are gay. I have always treated them with love and respect. My view of their behavior is not my view of them as human beings. It is no different from my view of someone having sex outside of marriage or someone committing adultery. I disapprove of their behavior, not them.

I do not believe that in terms of God's view, there are degrees of sin. It only takes one sin of any kind to separate us from God and prevent us from entering heaven. God's grace and forgiveness, once accepted, applies to any and every sin.

I do, however, believe that different sins have different effects and consequences, some more destructive than others. A lie does not have the same effect that murder does. I believe that homosexuality has severe consequences, not just individually but for society. I respect your right to disagree, but there is no reason to hate me simply because I believe that this is God's design and does not change.

Early in this book, when I talked about God's design, I used the example of the law of gravity and jumping from a ten-story building. If I was at the top of that building and someone told me he did not believe in gravity and was about to jump, I would do everything in my power to stop him. He might be mad at me because his belief was sincere. He might believe that I had no right to interfere. My efforts to stop him would not mean that I hate him; quite the contrary. It would be despicable of me if I did not try.

I hope we can agree that in a free society, this is simply a mutual dilemma.

Why is homosexuality not in God's design?
www.livingthatmattersbook.com/26.html

How should Christians view homosexuality?
www.livingthatmattersbook.com/27.html

Creators

In the chapter on relational values, I talked about two of the purposes of marriage: to reflect the image of God and to multiply that image through procreation. In a world that is becoming predominantly anticreation, the children of God need to be pro-creation by procreating. Being the Creator is one of the primary attributes of God. Made in His image, we have a natural instinct to create. Human beings know that creating life is the premiere way that we pass on our heritage.

When you carefully examine all of the Scripture passages that talk about creation, both directly and indirectly, you will discover a wonderful truth. God enjoys being the Creator. He took pleasure in creating the universe. He took pleasure in creating the earth. He takes pleasure in the creation of every human being. I believe this is the reason God not only perfectly designed male and female bodies for procreation, but designed that process to be extremely pleasurable.

Many religions teach that it is a sin to enjoy sex, and that sex is only for procreation and not for pleasure. It is precisely because sex is for procreation that it should be pleasurable. We reflect the image of God when we enjoy the act and process of creating.

There are some wonderful books on the subject of the joy of sex in marriage. Two classics are *Sheet Music* by Dr. Kevin Leman and *Intended for Pleasure* by Ed Wheat MD and Gaye Wheat.

Health Benefits of Sex

A good sex life is vital to good mental, physical, and emotional health. Conversely, the corruption and/or neglect of our sexuality is detrimental to our mental, physical, and emotional health. I will not discuss all of the health benefits here, but I will provide links for you to read more.

Since this value is about the compatibility of male and female bodies, I want to first point out that most research shows that the greatest health benefits come from male-female intercourse. Most studies hide that information deep for the sake of political correctness.

Another fact they try to hide is that the greatest benefits also come from unprotected sex. God designed sex to work within the confines of a monogamous relationship between a man and a woman in marriage. That is the only true safe sex. Although there are still some health benefits from sex outside of marriage, that must be weighed against the health risks from a promiscuous lifestyle.

The health benefits of married sex are numerous. I will only cover a few of them directly in this book and not in great detail. Of course I already talked about one of the most obvious. That is the pure joy, which recent studies have shown is an important factor for good health.

Having sex once or twice a week has been linked with higher levels of an antibody called immunoglobulin A, or IgA, which can protect you from getting colds and other infections.

A twenty-year-long British study showed that men who had sex two or more times a week were half as likely to have a fatal heart attack as men who had sex less than once a month.

During sex, the body produces a hormone called oxytocin. Known as the "love hormone," oxytocin escalation triggers the release of endorphins, your body's natural painkillers. Once the endorphins kick in, pain is numbed. You feel better for hours, sometimes even days, after sex. If you suffer from frequent headaches, arthritis, or other recurring pain, remember that the act of sex can reduce your level of pain, thanks to oxytocin.

Recent studies have given oxytocin a new nickname, the "moral molecule." These studies show that oxytocin may be responsible for trust, empathy, and other feelings that create a stable society. It is also believed that oxytocin creates a desire for attachment in relationships.

I do need to add that, although sexual intercourse is probably the best way to raise oxytocin levels, it is not the only way. Any skin-to-skin contact works. Hugs are also good and one of my favorites.

These studies have also shown that when you pray, it increases oxytocin levels. Ain't God good? (Sorry, have I mentioned I am from Arkansas?)

How?

By now you are used to me saying that this is not a how-to book. Nowhere in the book will that make you feel more frustrated than here. The how-to is very important, but until you fully embrace these values (your operating system), all of the how-to knowledge in the world will not have the right meaning.

Follow all of the links and book recommendations in this chapter. A good place to start learning the how-to of sexual values is on a Web site called *The Marriage Bed*. It has a good biblical foundation with some practical information and links to many other good resources. Warning: It is graphic and blunt but very helpful. Just make sure that as you are learning, you do not move too far from the values.

The Marriage Bed
www.livingthatmattersbook.com/28.html

More good articles on sexuality.
www.livingthatmattersbook.com/29.html

The Top Three Sexual Values

1. *My body does not belong to me; it belongs to God. It will either reflect or dishonor His glory.*

2. *Through sexuality a husband and wife reflect the glory and image of God to each other.*

3. *The male body and the female body are designed to become one flesh. They fit together to reflect the glory and image of God through creation.*

www.sexualitythatmatters.com

Chapter 5 to be continued …

CHAPTER 6

Financial Values

God's Design for Finances

In order to understand financial values or God's financial design, we must understand what is even meant by finance. I read this definition of *finance* on Wikipedia: "the study of how people allocate their assets over time under conditions of certainty and uncertainty."

That is good. But then it went on to say, "A key point in finance, which affects decisions, is the time value of money, which states that a unit of currency today is worth more than the same unit of currency tomorrow." This means that in our culture, the primary focus of finance is on money or currency.

We want to focus more on the first part of that definition, which is "assets." Looking at Wikipedia again, the definition of *assets* is "economic resources." It goes on to say, "Anything tangible or intangible that is capable of being owned or controlled to produce value and that is held to have positive economic value is considered an asset."

In other words, assets are basically anything that we, or anyone else, might assign value to. That assignment of value does not necessarily have to be objective. In fact, we might just as rightly refer to "assigned value" as "subjective value." We might say it like this: "The only true value of something is however much someone is willing to pay for it." It is like the old saying, "One man's junk is another man's treasure."

However, there are some things that have intrinsic value. *Intrinsic value* is the value something has in and of itself, regardless of whether I believe it is valuable or not. For example, air has intrinsic value because, whether we desire it or not, we all need it.

Some things have both intrinsic and assigned value, such as gold or gems. Gold or gems have always had value to someone and always will. However, the assigned value of gold or gems changes from culture to culture and generation to generation. While different types of clothing or shelter or food may have different assigned values, the fact of having food, clothing, and shelter will always have intrinsic value.

God is always more interested in intrinsic value than He is in assigned value. In the book of Acts, Peter and John met a man who had been lame from birth.

Then Peter said, "Silver or gold I do not have, but what I do have I give you. In the name of Jesus Christ of Nazareth, walk." Taking him by the right hand, he helped him up, and instantly the man's feet and ankles became strong. He jumped to his feet and began to walk. Then he went with

them into the temple courts, walking and jumping, and praising God. (Acts 3:6–8 NASB)

We can clearly see here that the intrinsic value of being able to walk was much greater than the assigned value of silver and gold.

I understand that the difference between intrinsic and assigned value is not always this clear. The key is to pay close attention to what God values.

These explanations may seem a bit complicated. I think they will make more sense by the end of the chapter. I bring them up so you can grasp the intent of this chapter. The Bible has a great deal to say about money and the management of money. That is not the focus of this chapter. There are many good Christian helps available for the management of money, such as Crown Financial Ministries and Dave Ramsey's Financial Peace University. I would also highly recommend Saddleback Church's financial seminar.

Dave Ramsey
www.livingthatmattersbook.com/30.html

Crown Financial
www.livingthatmattersbook.com/31.html

Saddleback Church
www.livingthatmattersbook.com/32.html

These are all good, and you really need to check them out. But the focus of this chapter, as with the whole book, is not on the how-to of finance. Rather, it is on understanding and coming to a place of belief in God's financial design. It is about changing the way we think about finances. If I can accomplish that through this chapter, then you will get much more benefit from these financial programs.

Financial Value 1
Nothing Belongs to Me;
Everything Belongs to God. I
Am a Steward of His Assets

This is the financial language translation for "It's not about me; it's about God." The whole of financial values could simply be a subheading under spiritual values, because financial values only have meaning in the context of living out the spiritual values.

To make a point, I used to say to people, "I do not believe you have a soul." After a pause to let them wrestle with that, I would then say, "You *are* a soul. You *have* a body."

The soul, which is eternal, is really who we are. It is created in the image of God. In order to function in the physical realm of the earth, we need physical bodies. That is why God took on flesh in order to accomplish what was necessary in this world.

The Bible says that this earthly body is corrupt and decaying. It instructs us how to properly care for it so that it might serve to accomplish our purpose on earth. But we are not to give nurture of the body greater importance than nurture of the soul.

But have nothing to do with worldly fables fit only for old women. On the other hand, discipline yourself for the purpose of godliness; for bodily discipline is only of little profit, but godliness is profitable for all things, since it holds promise for the present life and also for the life to come. (1 Timothy 4:7–8 NASB)

In much the same way, finances are a necessary vehicle for us to function in this world as we live out the spiritual values. But we are not to give nurture of our finances greater priority than nurture of living out the spiritual values.

Someday we will be separated from this earthly body because it will have no use in heaven. In the same way finances, useful on earth, will have no use in heaven. On earth we are to be stewards of God's assets. For ourselves, we are to store our treasure in heaven. This is another way of teaching us to have an eternal mind-set.

"Do not store up for yourselves treasures on earth, where moth and rust destroy, and where thieves break in and steal. But store up for yourselves treasures in heaven, where neither moth nor rust destroys, and where thieves do not break in or steal; for where your treasure is, there your heart will be also. (Matthew 6:19–21 NASB)

People often misquote Scripture as saying that money is the root of evil. Scripture actually says that the love of money is the issue because it diverts our focus from our real purpose.

For we have brought nothing into the world, so we cannot take anything out of it either. If we have food and covering, with these we shall be content. But those who want to get rich fall into temptation and a snare and many foolish and harmful desires which plunge men into ruin and destruction. For the love of money is a root of all sorts of evil, and some by longing for it have wandered away from the faith and pierced themselves with many griefs.

But flee from these things, you man of God, and pursue righteousness, godliness, faith, love, perseverance and gentleness. (1 Timothy 6:7–11 NASB)

If you are not convinced how important this correlation is between our view of finances and living out our spiritual values, then let us see what Jesus had to say about it.

For this reason I say to you, do not be worried about your life, as to what you will eat or what you will drink; nor for your body, as to what you will put on. Is not life more than food, and the body more than clothing? Look at the birds of the air, that they do not sow, nor reap nor gather into barns, and yet your heavenly Father feeds them. Are you not worth much more than they? And who of you by being worried can add a single hour to his life? And why are you worried about clothing? Observe how the lilies of the field grow; they do not toil nor do they spin, yet I say to you that not even Solomon in all his glory clothed himself like one of these. But if God so clothes the grass of the field, which is alive today and tomorrow is thrown into the furnace, will He not much more clothe you? You of little faith! Do not worry then, saying, 'What will we eat?' or 'What will we drink?' or 'What will we wear for clothing?' For the Gentiles eagerly seek all these things; for your heavenly Father knows that you need all these things. But seek first His kingdom and His righteousness, and all these things will be added to you. (Matthew 6:25–33 NASB)

Almost everyone I talk to is worried about their finances. When I question them in detail about their finances, I usually discover two things to be true. First, at the core, what they worry about boils down to food, clothing, and shelter—things we consider the "necessities of life." After all, that is why we work for a paycheck. In the language of our culture, the true signs of financial difficulty are not whether you have a cell phone or a nice car but whether you have food, clothing, and shelter.

The second thing I find is that the more we worry and the harder we work to provide food, clothing, and shelter, the greater our view and definition of "necessities" grows. In other words, the more we have, the more we want.

John Rockefeller was one of the wealthiest men of the early nineteen hundreds. One day he was asked, "How much money does it take to make a man happy?"

He replied, "Just a little bit more."

In Luke's version of Matthew 6, Jesus tells a parable to illustrate the truth and folly of this problem:

And He told them a parable, saying, "The land of a rich man was very productive. And he began reasoning to himself, saying, 'What shall I do, since I have no place to store my crops?' Then he said, 'This is what I will do: I will tear down my barns and build larger ones, and there I will store all my grain and my goods. And I will say to my soul, "Soul, you have many goods laid up for many years to come; take your ease, eat, drink and be merry."' But God said to him, 'You fool! This very night your soul is required of you; and now who will own what you have prepared?' So is the man who stores up treasure for himself, and is not rich toward God." (Luke 12:16–21 NASB)

Think about what Jesus is telling us. He has promised that if we will stay focused on His kingdom with an eternal mind-set, He will always take care of food, clothing, and shelter. We do not even need to think about it. This is living our spiritual values: commitment to God, commitment to the body, commitment to the world.

However, if we choose to take care of "these things," i.e., food, clothing, and shelter, to the neglect of His kingdom, it will never be enough. We will always need/want more.

Financial Freedom

This is a phrase we hear a lot in our culture. Everyone is striving for financial freedom. But what does that mean?

There are two popular views of what financial freedom means. The first says financial freedom is to be debt-free. I smile at that one because in essence it means you want to be at zero.

The other view makes more sense to me, but I believe it still falls short of what God intends. This view says that financial freedom is when I have the financial ability to do what I want, when I want, and where I want.

According to the Scripture passages that I have shared in this chapter, I find a different view of financial freedom. Financial freedom is when you never, ever, ever, ever, ever, ever, ever worry about money. It really has nothing to do with how much money you have or even how much debt you have. (No, I do not believe you should be in debt.) It has to do with contentment. Contentment is the opposite of worry.

Not that I speak from want, for I have learned to be content in whatever circumstances I am. I know how to get along with humble means, and I also know how to live in prosperity; in any and every circumstance I have learned the secret of being filled and going hungry, both of having abundance and suffering need. I can do all things through Him who strengthens me. (Philippians 4:11–13 NASB)

If we have food and covering, with these we shall be content. (1 Timothy 6:8)

Some see the glass half-full; some see it half-empty. I say there is too much glass there. You see, it is only half-empty or half-full relative to the glass. When we look at the glass, it becomes either a negative view, focused on what we don't have, or a positive view, focused on how close we are to getting what we think we should have.

Both of those views assume that if the glass is full, we will be content. Neither of those views will bring contentment. If we focus on appreciating the content apart from the container, then the content is always full. Contentment will not come when we have what we want but when we want what we have.

Paul said that whether he had a lot or a little, he was content. Appreciation of content equals contentment. Focusing on the unfilled container always equals discontent.

My friend, until you learn this about God's design, then it really does not matter how well you manage the assets God has entrusted you with. Until that point, you are trying to manage your assets instead of His assets.

Owners think very differently than stewards. A steward is a person who manages the assets of someone else. "Everything belongs to God; nothing belongs to me. I am a steward of His assets." If this is not your value, then you are not managing the assets. They are managing you.

Listen to how strongly Jesus states this. Your view of finances determines how you relate to His kingdom.

Do not store up for yourselves treasures on earth, where moth and rust destroy, and where thieves break in and steal. But store up for yourselves treasures in heaven, where neither moth nor rust destroys, and where thieves do not break in or steal; for where your treasure is, there your heart will be also. "The eye is the lamp of the body; so then if your eye is clear, your whole body will be full of light. But if your eye is bad, your whole body will be full of darkness. If then the light that is in you is darkness, how great is the darkness! "No one can serve two masters; for either he will hate the one and love the other, or he will be devoted to one and despise the other. You cannot serve God and wealth. (Mathew 6:19–24 NASB)

This is beautifully illustrated in a sermon by Pastor John Ortberg: "When the game is over, it all goes back in the box."

Monopoly-back in the box
www.livingthatmattersbook.com/33.html

If this is truly your value, your understanding of God's design for finances, then all of the many passages in the Bible about managing finances will take on new meaning and help you to be a good steward. I hope you will check out some of the resources I have listed, but first let this value sink in.

This principle of contentment is learned through the financial values, but it affects every area of our lives. When we trust God for food, clothing, and shelter, we trust Him for everything.

When the Israelites were afraid to enter the Promised Land, because they were afraid of the giants, it showed that they did not trust God. God brought them to a place where food, clothing, and shelter were in abundance, but their eyes told them that they could not receive it because of the giants. So God led them through the wilderness to teach them that they could trust Him. He taught them by making them totally dependent on Him for food, clothing, and shelter. At the end of the forty years, this is what He told them:

You shall remember all the way which the Lord your God has led you in the wilderness these forty years, that He might humble you, testing you, to know what was in your heart, whether you would keep His commandments or not. He humbled you and let you be hungry, and fed you with manna which you did not know, nor did your fathers know, that He might make you understand that man does not live by bread alone, but man lives by everything that proceeds out of the mouth of the Lord. Your clothing did not wear out on you, nor did your foot swell these forty years. Thus you are to know in your heart that the Lord your God was disciplining you just as a man disciplines his son. Therefore, you shall keep the commandments of the

Lord your God, to walk in His ways and to fear Him. For the Lord your God is bringing you into a good land, a land of brooks of water, of fountains and springs, flowing forth in valleys and hills; a land of wheat and barley, of vines and fig trees and pomegranates, a land of olive oil and honey; a land where you will eat food without scarcity, in which you will not lack anything; a land whose stones are iron, and out of whose hills you can dig copper. When you have eaten and are satisfied, you shall bless the Lord your God for the good land which He has given you. "Beware that you do not forget the Lord your God by not keeping His commandments and His ordinances and His statutes which I am commanding you today; otherwise, when you have eaten and are satisfied, and have built good houses and lived in them, and when your herds and your flocks multiply, and your silver and gold multiply, and all that you have multiplies, then your heart will become proud and you will forget the Lord your God who brought you out from the land of Egypt, out of the house of slavery. He led you through the great and terrible wilderness, with its fiery serpents and scorpions and thirsty ground where there was no water; He brought water for you out of the rock of flint. In the wilderness He fed you manna which your fathers did not know, that He might humble you and that He might test you, to do good for you in the end. (Deuteronomy 8:2–16 NASB)

He warned them that if they ever forgot how He provided them with food, clothing, and shelter, they would become proud, wanting more and more above and beyond necessities. That would distract them from what life is really about. I cannot stress enough how important this financial value is to our spiritual values.

Otherwise, you may say in your heart, 'My power and the strength of my hand made me this wealth.' But you shall remember the Lord your God, for it is He who is giving you power to make wealth, that He may confirm His covenant which He swore to your fathers, as it is this day. It shall come about if you ever forget the Lord your God and go after other gods and serve them and worship them, I testify against you today that you will surely perish. Like the nations that the Lord makes to perish before you, so you shall perish; because you would not listen to the voice of the Lord your God.

Once we are truly living this first value, then we can begin to understand the next value. It is a very difficult value to articulate, as it is more a mind-set than it is a tangible way of doing things.

Financial Value 2
The World Operates on a System of Buying and Selling; God Operates on a System of Giving and Receiving

In order to grasp this value, I must first make clear that the giving referred to in this value is not exclusively the giving of tithes and offerings to God. The giving of tithes and offerings reveals how well we understand the first value. Giving God His tithe reveals that we know that He is the owner and gets the first fruits of everything. Giving to God our offerings reveals that we understand that everything we have comes from Him and will be continually replenished by Him.

This all teaches us that God is the owner and we are the stewards of His assets. I stated earlier that stewards think very differently than owners do, especially if you are steward for an owner with unlimited assets. The difference between buying and selling and giving and receiving is a difference of mind-set, not simply a difference of action.

Both of these systems may involve the exchange of one asset for another (e.g., money for a product). In the system of buying and selling, the highest goal of the trade is that it be an equitable trade. In other words, the seller and the buyer are to end up with assets of equal value, even if it is only a perceived/subjective value.

When you live in financial freedom or contentment, all assets take on a quality of intrinsic value. This is because they come from a limitless source. When you give one asset of intrinsic value, you receive another asset that then takes on intrinsic value. You cannot lose. You cannot be cheated. This is so true that Jesus tells us not to fight it even if it appears we are being cheated.

Give to everyone who asks of you, and whoever takes away what is yours, do not demand it back. (Luke 6:30)

No one can take from us what we freely give. I can only freely give in this way when I recognize that what I am giving does not belong to me in the first place. I am following the instruction from the owner on how to manage it. Jesus Himself practiced this value even to the point of giving His life. He said no one could take it from Him, but He gave it freely.

Recently, I came home from the doctor with some new, very expensive medication to help prevent my cluster headaches. My wife asked me how much it cost. When I told her, she said, "Wow, for that price it had sure better work." I understood what she meant, but I told her that in reality, one has nothing to do with the other. The medicine was worth a try to me regardless of the price, and its ability to work had nothing to do with the price. If it did not work, I would not have wasted or lost the money. The fact that I had the money and that it was the right thing to try the medicine was all a gift from God. When you operate in a system of giving and receiving, this becomes your mind-set for every financial transaction.

I stated before that this value is very difficult to articulate. I know that there are some of you reading this who are practical thinkers and have been through some good training on biblical financial management. You will say to me, "This simply sounds like a license to spend money any way that you want and then just say the results don't matter as long as I have a mind-set of giving and receiving."

I assure you that this is not what I am saying. I want to say, like Paul the apostle said when faced with this type of response, "May it not never be!" (My autocorrect didn't like that statement, but the double negative that Paul used also expresses my point.) You still need to follow biblical principles of financial management. But when you have this mind-set, you can follow those principles with freedom from worry or regret.

This is not an excuse to be frivolous with your finances. However, I think sometimes the financial disciplines we learn in Christian seminars can be an excuse to trust our management and not God's provisions. (I want to make clear that I would not recommend those seminars if I did not believe in them. I do believe in them.)

Let me give you an example that I am sure will draw lots of criticism. I believe in the "ten-ten-eighty" principle: tithe 10 percent of your income first, pay 10 percent to your savings, and then live on the remaining 80 percent. I also believe that it is wise to save for retirement, separate from your other savings.

However, if I believe God is directing me in some area that will require me to spend or give money that He has not provided from any other source, I have no problem using my savings or my retirement fund. Several years ago my church had a building campaign. They asked for pledges to be given over a three-year period. My wife and I prayed and came up with an impossible amount to pledge.

Shortly after that, my income was cut dramatically. Over the next two years, in spite of being very tight financially, we were faithful to give the amount pledged. When the third year came due, according to our pledge, we simply did not have the money. We prayed and waited but it did not come. We joyfully took the money from my retirement account and gave it to God as promised. I am not worried in the least about my retirement, though I will continue to look for wise ways to plan for it.

It will be much easier to understand this value if we take it out of the context of money. I discussed in the beginning of the chapter that money or currency is only one kind of asset. Giving and receiving applies to every kind of asset, both tangible and intangible.

Give, and it will be given to you. They will pour into your lap a good measure-pressed down, shaken together, and running over. For by your standard of measure it will be measured to you in return. (Luke 6:38 NASB)

This passage is almost always taught in the context of money, but it is unlikely that money is what Jesus had in mind. All of the surrounding verses talk about how we are to treat people, especially our enemies or those who treat us wrongly. It clearly shows that we are not to give simply to get equal value back. It is saying that when we receive "bad" from someone, we are to give "good." This good negates the bad.

So verse 38 is not just referring to money but also to the way we treat people. When we give with intrinsic value, we will get back with that same standard of measure.

Another view we get of the value of giving and receiving comes from the laws of the harvest or the laws of sowing and reaping. I equate sowing and reaping with giving and receiving. God expects us to invest the assets that He has entrusted to us. If we do not understand these laws, it will often seem like we are not receiving according to the same standard of measure that we give, and we will be discouraged and lose heart.

Do not be deceived, God is not mocked; for whatever a man sows, this he will also reap. For the one who sows to his own flesh will from the flesh reap corruption, but the one who sows to the Spirit will from the Spirit reap eternal life. Let us not lose heart in doing good, for in due time we will reap if we do not grow weary. So then, while we have opportunity, let us do good to all people, and

especially to those who are of the household of the faith. (Galatians 6:7–10 NASB)

The first law of the harvest is that *we will reap/receive what we sow/give.* When you plant apple seeds, you get apples. If you plant/give love, you get love. If you plant/give hate, you get hate. Whatever it is that you sow, good or bad, that is what you reap.

The second law of the harvest is that *we always reap/receive more than we sow/give.* The truth is that when you plant an apple seed, you don't just get an apple—you get an apple tree with lots of apples.

When I was young, parents would refer to teenagers who were misbehaving as simply "sowing their wild oats." If that is true, then someday they will be praying for a crop failure because the harvest of those wild oats will not be pleasant. You may have heard it said that what one generation does in moderation, the next generation will do in excess.

These first two laws are fairly easy to grasp. We can see how they can benefit us if we are sowing/giving good things. The third law is more difficult. If we do not understand it, we will be discouraged in our giving.

The third law of the harvest is that *we always reap/receive later than we sow/give.* You do not put an apple seed in the ground and wake up in the morning to see an apple tree. It takes time. It also sometimes takes watering and spreading some fertilizer before the harvest comes. It may be that when you truly learn to give, you will go through a lot of manure before seeing the fruit of your giving.

At the root of the harvest is planting, which I have compared with giving. Just as you cannot reap if you do not plant, you cannot receive if you do not give. Matthew 6 does not say "Receive, and because you receive you should give." The process is to give, and because you give it will be given to you. We should not give in order to receive, but we will definitely receive because we give. Giving and receiving must become as natural as inhaling and exhaling.

There is another point that needs to be made about this value of giving and receiving. When you develop this mind-set, it will also affect the way that you work. The Bible says, *"If a man will not work he should not eat" (2 Thessalonians 3:10).* It also says, *"A man who does not provide for his own household is worse than an unbeliever" (1 Timothy 5:8).* We work in order to receive an income so we can provide for our families. We must see work as something we give not simply to get an income, but because it is the right thing to do.

Whatever you do, do your work heartily, as for the Lord rather than for men, knowing that from the Lord you will receive the reward of the inheritance. It is the Lord Christ whom you serve. (Colossians 3:23–24)

The difference this makes is the same difference we talked about earlier concerning buying and selling. We are not looking for an equitable trade because God makes it all equitable. When you work "as for the Lord," you will work with the same passion whether you are being paid minimum wage or the top salary. When you see your work as giving, then you will always receive much more than wages. Your earnings will be "pressed down, shaken together, overflowing." Your employer may cheat you, but you will always reap the true fruit of your labor.

Because of this mind-set, I can honestly say that I have never truly been unemployed. When I do not have a job, then I consider finding a job to be my job. I work at it with the same passion "as for the Lord," and I always reap a plentiful harvest.

Financial Value 3
Living in the Body of Christ
Is True Communism

I need to ask you once again to set aside your presuppositions. When you see the word *communism*, it probably has a negative connotation for you. After all, every experiment in communism has failed, hasn't it?

Well, the major, famous cases have indeed failed. China, the Soviet Union, and East Germany are all examples of why communism does not work. In each of these cases, communism was a political venture. It was mandated and managed by the government.

Why did these examples fail? The truth is that most of what Marx and Engels wrote in "The Communist Manifesto" would be true if it were not for one major flaw. All of it is based on one foundational belief, and the success of the system hinges on whether or not this foundational belief is true. Marx and Engels believed that all human beings are basically good at heart, and if given a fair and equal opportunity, they will live in unity. We know from the Bible that this is far from the truth. We know that mankind is sinful by nature. Without a change of heart, mankind will always end up doing the wrong thing.

It may surprise you to know that there is an example, an overlooked example, in history of successful communism. It is called the body of Christ, the people of the Way, the family of God, and the church of Jesus Christ.

Before reading further, go back to the chapter on spiritual values and read again the section on commitment to the body. This is another example of how the financial values support the spiritual values.

To understand how communism can work, you must understand that the church is not an organization but an organism. It does not operate like a government but as a family. The church of Jesus Christ is not a democracy. It is a theocracy. It is the only system in the world in which there can truly be equality.

The original intent of communism was to end the class structure and make all people equal. But because communism is, by its very nature, a forced philosophy, it is destined to failure. Evil men will always find a way to control it.

In the church of Jesus Christ, there is but one class—royalty! We are all children of the King.

For all of you who were baptized into Christ have clothed yourselves with Christ. There is neither Jew nor Greek, there is neither slave nor free man, there is neither male nor female; for you are all one in Christ Jesus. And if you belong to Christ, then you are Abraham's descendants, heirs according to promise. (Galatians 3:27–29 NASB)

This is true equality and can never be diminished by governments or laws or social status. When we truly understand this, then it will not only change our view of ourselves but of each other. We are joint heirs. This governs how we relate to each other. My brother in Christ may be my employee, but I am to treat him as a joint heir, a fellow child of the King.

You are probably thinking, "That all sounds great, but I sure do not see the church working that way." You are right. One of the reasons I am writing this book is that, sadly, the church has moved very far away from God's design. Most churches today operate on a system that more closely resembles a business or government model than the biblical model. This is in part because of a misunderstanding of three passages of Scripture.

Submit yourselves for the Lord's sake to every human institution, whether to a king as the one in authority, or to governors as sent by him for the punishment of evildoers and the praise of those who do right. For such is the will of God that by doing right you may silence the ignorance of foolish men. (1 Peter 2:13–15)

Every person is to be in subjection to the governing authorities. For there is no authority except from God, and those which exist are established by God. Therefore whoever resists authority has opposed the ordinance of God; and they who have opposed will receive condemnation upon themselves.

These first two passages clearly tell us to submit to the government and every human institution. But we have completely blown this out of context. We have allowed the government to act as a higher authority than Scripture.

A great example of this is in the marriage controversy we see today. How is it that we ever thought it was all right for the government to define marriage in the first place? Marriage was never designed to be a civil institution or a legal contract. If people really understood what a marriage license legally does, they would be horrified.

Marriage License
www.livingthatmattersbook.com/34.html

The point is that this is one small illustration of how we have allowed the government and society, rather than the Bible, to influence church structure. These passages were never intended to promote this view; otherwise Peter would be sinning in the following passage.

When they had brought them, they stood them before the Council. The high priest questioned them, saying, "We gave you strict orders not to continue teaching in this name, and yet, you have filled Jerusalem with your teaching and intend to bring this man's blood upon us."

***But Peter and the apostles answered, "We must obey God
rather than men." (Acts 5:27–29)***

The third Scripture passage about government is taken even
further out of context. Misunderstanding of this passage has
developed into a false philosophy of how the church is to
relate to the world. It is appropriate to look at it here since
this is, after all, a chapter on financial values.

Versions of the passage are found in three of the gospels:
Matthew 22:15–22; Mark 12:13–17; and Luke 20:20–26. I
am only showing the Luke passage here.

***They questioned Him, saying, "Teacher, we know that
You speak and teach correctly, and You are not partial
to any, but teach the way of God in truth. Is it lawful
for us to pay taxes to Caesar, or not?" But He detected
their trickery and said to them, "Show Me a denarius.
Whose likeness and inscription does it have?" They said,
"Caesar's." And He said to them, "Then render to Caesar
the things that are Caesar's, and to God the things that
are God's." And they were unable to catch Him in a saying
in the presence of the people; and being amazed at His
answer, they became silent. (Luke 20:21–26 NASB)***

This story is used to justify any and every submission to or
cooperation with the world's systems, even if those systems
are not in harmony with Scripture. It is amazing how many
different ways this passage is applied to justify policies.

I was recently in a conversation with the leader of a large
church. We were talking about marriage and divorce. I
showed him Scripture that clearly stated a different view
of marriage and divorce than his church policies, which are

based on a legal view in harmony with cultural norms. He actually cited this passage from Luke as a defense of why his church follows the system and policies they do rather than the biblical verses I showed him. He never once said that I was interpreting those verses wrongly.

Without going into an exegesis of this passage, let me use three quotations that express how I think we should approach this. I do not agree with everything these men believed, but I do agree with these statements.

Mennonite pastor John K. Stoner spoke for those who interpret the parable as permitting or even encouraging tax resistance: "We are war tax resisters because we have discovered some doubt as to what belongs to Caesar and what belongs to God, and have decided to give the benefit of the doubt to God."

Tertullian, in *De Idololatria*, interprets Jesus as saying to render "the image of Caesar, which is on the coin, to Caesar, and the image of God, which is on man, to God; so as to render to Caesar indeed money, to God yourself. Otherwise, what will be God's, if all things are Caesar's?"

Leo Tolstoy wrote:

> Not only the complete misunderstanding of Christ's teaching, but also a complete unwillingness to understand it could have admitted that striking misinterpretation, according to which the words, "To Cæsar the things which are Cæsar's," signify the necessity of obeying Cæsar. In the first place, there is no mention there of obedience; in the second place, if Christ recognized the obligatoriness

of paying tribute, and so of obedience, He would have said directly, "Yes, it should be paid;" but He says, "Give to Cæsar what is his, that is, the money, and give your life to God," and with these latter words He not only does not encourage any obedience to power, but, on the contrary, points out that in everything which belongs to God it is not right to obey Cæsar.

Before I get too far off track, let me make clear that I am looking at these passages in the context of why and how the church is not following the biblical model of what the church is to be.

Now, let's look at what the church is supposed to be, especially in relationship to this financial value: "Living in the body of Christ is true communism." In the chapter on relational values, I already showed the difference between equality of value and equality of function. Men and women, just like the trinity, are equal in value but not equal in function. This is where Marxist communism and biblical communism differ. Marxist communism is based on fairness, but biblical communism is based on justice.

Here is a great article on the difference between fairness and justice.

Fairness vs. Justice
www.livingthatmattersbook.com/35.html

Biblical communism is a natural response of *justice* to genuine need. Marxist communism is a forced reaction to bring *fairness* to perceived greed. Biblical communism builds up while Marxist communism tears down.

Let me illustrate this for you. Suppose I was teaching a class with twenty students in it. Suppose that it is known in the class that I am the only one who knows how to give CPR. Now suppose one of the students fell on the floor, having a heart attack. I know exactly what needs to be done and begin giving him CPR.

Suddenly the others students begin complaining. "Mr. Lewis, this is not fair. Why does he get CPR and we don't?"

Well, there is one of me able to give it, he needs it, and you don't. It is just that simple. It is a just thing for me to give him CPR and not the rest of the class.

Now that sounds silly, doesn't it? But it is just as silly when we try to live in communism based on fairness and not justice.

The Bible clearly tells us that every member of the body of Christ has equal value but not equal function. This relationship of value and function is the foundation on which true communism can be built.

For just as we have many members in one body and all the members do not have the same function, so we, who are many, are one body in Christ, and individually members one of another. Since we have gifts that differ according to the grace given to us, each of us is to exercise them accordingly: if prophecy, according to the proportion of his faith; if service, in his serving; or he who teaches, in his teaching; or he who exhorts, in his exhortation; he who gives, with liberality; he who leads, with diligence; he who shows mercy, with cheerfulness.

Let love be without hypocrisy. Abhor what is evil; cling to what is good. Be devoted to one another in brotherly love; give preference to one another in honor; not lagging behind in diligence, fervent in spirit, serving the Lord; rejoicing in hope, persevering in tribulation, devoted to prayer, contributing to the needs of the saints, practicing hospitality. (Romans 12:4–13 NASB)

I realize that I have made some very bold statements here. I hope that you have been able to, as I asked, set aside your presuppositions as to what communism is. But now it is time for me to back up my statements with Scripture, which clearly shows that the early church lived in true communism.

They were continually devoting themselves to the apostles' teaching and to fellowship, to the breaking of bread and to prayer. Everyone kept feeling a sense of awe; and many wonders and signs were taking place through the apostles. And all those who had believed were together and had all things in common; and they began selling their property and possessions and were sharing them with all, as anyone might have need. Day by day continuing with one mind in the temple, and breaking bread from house to house, they were taking their meals together with gladness and sincerity of heart, praising God and having favor with all the people. And the Lord was adding to their number day by day those who were being saved. (Acts 2:42–47 NASB)

And the congregation of those who believed were of one heart and soul; and not one of them claimed that anything belonging to him was his own, but all things were common property to them. And with great power the apostles were giving testimony to the resurrection of the Lord Jesus, and abundant grace was upon them all. For there was not a needy person among them, for all who were owners of land or houses would sell them and bring the proceeds of the sales and lay them at the apostles' feet, and they would be distributed to each as any had need.

Now Joseph, a Levite of Cyprian birth, who was also called Barnabas by the apostles (which translated means Son of Encouragement), and who owned a tract of land, sold it and brought the money and laid it at the apostles' feet. (Acts 4:32–37 NASB)

Maybe it's just me, but that sure sounds like communism.

The result of this is found in verse 34: "***There was not a needy person among them.***" The key to this is that no one told them to live this way. It happened naturally because they were behaving like family. This was the way that God's people were supposed to be behaving all along, but their hearts had become hardened.

I stated at the beginning of the book that I believe God's laws are His human articulation of His design. Look at the instructions God gave His people in Deuteronomy for how they were to live in the Promised Land.

"If there is a poor man with you, one of your brothers, in any of your towns in your land which the Lord your God is giving you, you shall not harden your heart, nor close your hand from your poor brother; but you shall freely open your hand to him, and shall generously lend him

sufficient for his need in whatever he lacks. Beware that there is no base thought in your heart, saying, 'The seventh year, the year of remission, is near,' and your eye is hostile toward your poor brother, and you give him nothing; then he may cry to the Lord against you, and it will be a sin in you. You shall generously give to him, and your heart shall not be grieved when you give to him, because for this thing the Lord your God will bless you in all your work and in all your undertakings. For the poor will never cease to be in the land; therefore I command you, saying, 'You shall freely open your hand to your brother, to your needy and poor in your land." (Deuteronomy 15:7–11 NASB)

In my first year of marriage, I was a struggling college student in Riverside, California. I was working part-time as a worship leader in a church that was an hour's drive from school. I drove a beat-up old car with bald tires.

One Sunday after church, I was walking to my car to drive back to school. There was an incredible older man in the church, named Tom Corn. All the kids loved him, and everyone affectionately called him Popcorn. He noticed my bald tires and began to lecture me that it was not safe to drive on them. I explained that I had no choice as I could not afford new tires. He told me to get in my car and follow him. He took me to a tire store and paid for brand-new tires for my car.

I was embarrassed and amazed and grateful. I fumbled for the right words, asking him why he would do such a thing. I will never forget what he said. "It is very simple. You need tires but cannot afford them. I don't need tires but I can afford them. This is how families behave. This is what church is all about."

I made the statement earlier that for true communism to work, there must be a change of heart. That is why I would never want to live under a communist government or a communist society outside of the church. The heart change necessary for natural communism happens when we yield all our rights to God. Read that section again in chapter 1.

Let's look again at the Scripture passages I used there.

Make my joy complete by being of the same mind, maintaining the same love, united in spirit, intent on one purpose. (Philippians 2:2 NASB)

This is the foundation for true and biblical communism. Without these four things in common—mind, love, spirit, and purpose—there can be nothing else in common. How does this happen?

Do nothing from selfishness or empty conceit, but with humility of mind regard one another as more important than yourselves; do not merely look out for your own personal interests, but also for the interests of others. Have this attitude in yourselves which was also in Christ Jesus. (Philippians 2:3–5 NASB)

I heard a story about a woman who had a dream revealing the difference between heaven and hell. In the first part of the dream, she saw hell. Everyone was seated around a huge banquet table laid with an amazing feast. Each person had one hand tied behind his or her back, and to the other hand was tied a four-foot-long spoon. The place was a mess as they tried to eat but could not get any food into their mouths. In spite of this huge feast, they were starving.

Then her dream switched to heaven. Here was a similar scene. Everyone was seated around a banquet table laid with an amazing feast. Each person had one hand tied behind his or her back and the other hand tied to a four-foot-long spoon. There was one difference in this scene—they were feeding each other.

It is just a story, but it does illustrate what should be the heart of God's family.

This voluntary, free sharing did not just take place in that first church in Jerusalem. I don't have room to post the entire passage here, but if you will read 2 Corinthians chapters 8 and 9, you will see that this pattern was consistent throughout the body of Christ as the church spread throughout the world. This was the result of that lifestyle:

For the ministry of this service is not only fully supplying the needs of the saints, but is also overflowing through many thanksgivings to God. Because of the proof given by this ministry, they will glorify God for your obedience to your confession of the gospel of Christ and for the liberality of your contribution to them and to all, while they also, by prayer on your behalf, yearn for you because of the surpassing grace of God in you. Thanks be to God for His indescribable gift! (2 Corinthians 9:12–15 NASB)

This brings up an important aspect of this value that should be highlighted. We are to care about the needs of the whole world. That is not what this value is about; however, the natural result is that it spills over into the world.

So then, while we have opportunity, let us do good to all people, and especially to those who are of the household of the faith. (Galatians 6:10)

Anyone who flies on a regular basis can probably quote the safety speech given before every flight. The flight attendant says that in the case of the cabin becoming depressurized, an oxygen mask will drop down in front of you. It is very important that if you have young children or elderly traveling companions, you must put your own oxygen mask on first before you help them. If you do not, you will probably both die because you will pass out before you are able to help them.

If we cannot care about our own family, how will the world believe we care about them? If our people are in need, why would the world believe we are able to meet its needs?

When the body of Christ is healthy and thriving, it will draw the world in. They will want what we have. As we saw in Acts, this "communist" lifestyle led them to a place of *"praising God and having favor with all the people. And the Lord was adding to their number day by day those who were being saved" (Acts 2:47 NASB).*

This will always be the result. Remember the value from chapter 2: *We are designed to be part of His body, the church.*

"A new commandment I give to you, that you love one another, even as I have loved you, that you also love one another. "By this all men will know that you are My disciples, if you have love for one another." (John 13:34–35 NASB-U)

Please do not think that I am telling you that you have to sell everything you have and for everyone to be equally poor. As with all of these values, this is a mind-set. It is not about bringing everyone down to the same level. It is realizing that when one part of the body hurts, the whole body is affected.

So now we have seen that each of the financial values is designed to help us fulfill the spiritual values. I hope you have a new mind-set about finances, one that shows it is all about God.

How?

I hope you will avail yourself of the many financial resources I have recommended in this chapter. There is more Scripture about financial management in the Bible than perhaps any other topic, so it must be very important.

My hope and prayer is that in working hard to be a good manager, you will not forget God's design for how we view finances—not just money, but rather all assets. On the Web sites, www.parentingthatmatters.org and www.financethatmatters.com, I will also make resources available for how to teach these financial designs to your children and how to leave a financial legacy.

It is vitally important in all five value categories, but especially this one, that you start with your "why." Learning the "what" and the "how" of financial management might make you prosper in the world's eyes, but if you do not have the right "why," you will have greatly missed the mark in God's eyes.

Start with your why.
www.livingthatmattersbook.com/36.html

....

The Top Three Financial Values

1. *Everything belongs to God; nothing belongs to me. I am a steward of His assets.*

2. *The world operates on a system of buying and selling. God operates on a system of giving and receiving.*

3. *Living in the body of Christ is true communism.*

www.financethatmatters.com

Chapter 6 to be continued...

CHAPTER 7

Grace, Mercy, and Planned Failure

Throughout the book, I have used many computer metaphors. I have compared our value system to the operating system on a computer. Conviction is a program that God puts on our hard drives to let us know if everything is working according to design.

But, just like on a computer, we can get malware that corrupts the function of the operating system. Some are fairly harmless but others are viruses that can seriously damage the operating system. Among the slickest types of viruses are ones that pretend to help you. You get a message that pops up saying that a scan has found serious threats on your computer and you should "click here" to let the software fix it before it is too late. You click and discover that either they are trying to sell you something or, worse, they are able to gain access to your computer without you knowing it.

I believe that one of Satan's favorite malware programs is a virus called guilt. It pretends to be from God. It is usually like a Trojan horse, often using Scripture to sneak past our filters. When guilt takes over, it blocks our relationship with God and prevents real growth. It distorts our view and understanding of Scripture and is the biggest cause for losing heart.

Godly Conviction versus Satanic Guilt

So now you have read the book and understand God's design. Everything in your life should be working perfectly … *not!* Wouldn't it be nice if it were that easy?

The reality is that you probably understand the design just enough to make you feel guilty for not following it. Guilt is the greatest enemy of growing to maturity. Guilt reveals that we have not fully embraced the first and foremost value expressed in this book: "It's not about me; it's about God." Guilt shows that I believe it *is* all about me.

The Bible says that King David was "a man after God's own heart" (Acts 13:22). That is a very confusing statement in light of some of David's actions. David committed adultery with Bathsheba, and then when she became pregnant, he murdered her husband. This is the man who was after God's own heart? How can this be?

To understand this, we need to first look at the statement a little differently. The reason David was a man after God's own heart was because David was after the heart of God. David was a great sinner, but he was also a great confessor. I encourage you to become very familiar with the entire Psalm

51. It is in this prayer that we can see David's heart for God in relationship to his sin.

> *Create in me a clean heart, O God,*
> *And renew a steadfast spirit within me.*
> *Do not cast me away from Your presence*
> *And do not take Your Holy Spirit from me.*
> *Restore to me the joy of Your salvation*
> *And sustain me with a willing spirit.*
> *Then I will teach transgressors Your ways,*
> *And sinners will be converted to You.*
> *Deliver me from bloodguiltiness, O God, the*
> *God of my salvation;*
> *Then my tongue will joyfully sing of Your*
> *righteousness.*
> *O Lord, open my lips,*
> *That my mouth may declare Your praise.*
> *For You do not delight in sacrifice, otherwise I*
> *would give it;*
> *You are not pleased with burnt offering.*
> *The sacrifices of God are a broken spirit;*
> *A broken and a contrite heart, O God, You will*
> *not despise. (Psalm 51:10–17 NASB)*

Verses 16 and 17 are the key. Guilt makes me want to offer sacrifice to atone for my sin. When my heart is truly broken over my sin, I realize that He alone, through His sacrifice, can atone for my sin. Satanic guilt focuses on me and how bad I am. Godly conviction causes me to focus on how good God is.

In Psalm 32, David tells the story behind Psalm 51.

> *How blessed is he who never transgresses,*
> *Who never sins!*
> *How blessed is the man who has no iniquity,*

Wait a minute! Oops … My satanic autocorrect misprinted that Scripture! Let's try again.

> *How blessed is he whose transgression is forgiven,*
> *Whose sin is covered!*
> *How blessed is the man to whom the Lord does*
> *not impute iniquity, And in whose spirit there*
> *is no deceit! (Psalm 32:1–2 NASB)*

Scripture does not say we will be happy because we never sin. In fact the implication here is that it is a given that we *will* sin. Romans 3:23 says we all have sinned and come short of God's glory. Happiness comes when our hearts are honest with God about our sin so that He can free us.

> *When I kept silent about my sin, my body wasted*
> *away*
> *Through my groaning all day long.*
> *For day and night Your hand was heavy upon me;*
> *My vitality was drained away as with the fever*
> *heat of summer. Selah.*
> *I acknowledged my sin to You,*
> *And my iniquity I did not hide;*
> *I said, "I will confess my transgressions to the*
> *Lord";*
> *And You forgave the guilt of my sin. Selah.*
> *(Psalm 32:3–5)*

There is that word *Selah* again. Stop and meditate on this.

This is such a profound statement. It does not simply say, "God forgave my sin." It says He forgave the *guilt* of my sin. This statement terrifies the kingdom of hell. When Jesus was on the cross, He cried out, "It is finished!" The work of atonement was done. The price had been paid. In this statement, Satan loses his power over us. This does not make him a happy camper.

In 1971, I went to a drive-in movie with my wife. (You youngsters will have to Google that to see what a drive-in is.) We saw a movie called *Dirty Harry* starring Clint Eastwood. It was a story about a serial killer in San Francisco called the Zodiac Killer.

At one point in the movie, the killer kidnapped a young girl and buried her in a box with a limited amount of oxygen. Then he taunted the police to find her before it ran out. Detective Harry captured the man and tortured him to get him to tell the location. When the police found where she was buried, they also found lots of evidence, including videos of the murders the killer committed. When he went on trial, his lawyers showed that all of that evidence had been obtained through illegal torture and was therefore inadmissible. The judge was forced to dismiss the case for lack of evidence. The horns of every car at the theater were honking and people were literally screaming at the screen because they were so upset at this injustice. We were angry that this guilty man was allowed to go free on a technicality.

At the heavenly courthouse, Satan brings charges against us—charges that are just. He offers irrefutable evidence against us. We are guilty and the penalty is death.

My little children, I am writing these things to you so that you may not sin. And if anyone sins, we have an Advocate with the Father, Jesus Christ the righteous; and He Himself is the propitiation for our sins; and not for ours only, but also for those of *the whole world. (1 John 2:1–2 NASB)*

Then our lawyer, Jesus Christ (in the verse above, the word *advocate* means "lawyer"), stands to show that all of that evidence against us is inadmissible because the penalty has already been paid. Satan is furious. He has lost. He immediately goes to plan B. If he cannot convict us in God's court, he will convict us in our own minds. He holds us captive through guilt and shame, and we become ineffective in living God's purpose in our lives. Psalm 32 is about breaking that bondage and living in freedom.

Here is how you can tell the difference between godly conviction and satanic guilt. Godly conviction always leads to victory and freedom. Satanic guilt always leads to defeat and slavery. It is the difference between Romans 7 and Romans 8.

Slavery and Defeat

Romans 7

But I see a different law in the members of my body, waging war against the law of my mind and making me a prisoner of the law of sin which is in my members. Wretched man that I am! Who will set me free from the body of this death? (Romans 7:23–24 NASB)

Victory and Freedom

Romans 8

For you have not received a spirit of slavery leading to fear again, but you have received a spirit of adoption as sons by which we cry out, "Abba! Father!" The Spirit Himself testifies with our spirit that we are children of God, and if children, heirs also, heirs of God and fellow heirs with Christ. (Romans 8:15–17 NASB)

Condemnation versus Forgiveness

One of the effects of guilt is that it not only distorts our view of ourselves but it also distorts our view of others. Guilt causes us to compare ourselves to others. The better they look, the worse we look. We often try to remedy this by either influencing them to come down to our level or condemning them, acting as Satan's voice to fill them with guilt.

One of the things that malicious viruses do on our computers is to infiltrate our contacts list and send out messages as if from us, infecting the computers of our friends. This is the same effect that guilt often has in our relationships. This is how the virus spreads throughout the body of Christ.

We should be helping our brothers and sisters to be free. When they are caught up in sin, we should tell them so in love. When they wrong us, we should forgive. But we cannot do this if we ourselves are in bondage.

"Do not judge so that you will not be judged. For in the way you judge, you will be judged; and by your standard of measure, it will be measured to you. Why do you look at the speck that is in your brother's eye, but do not notice the log that is in your own eye? Or how can you say to your brother, 'Let me take the speck out of your eye,' and behold, the log is in your own eye? You hypocrite, first take the log out of your own eye, and then you will see clearly to take the speck out of your brother's eye." (Matthew 7:1–5 NASB)

Brethren, even if anyone is caught in any trespass, you who are spiritual, restore such a one in a spirit of gentleness; each one looking to yourself, so that you too will not be tempted. Bear one another's burdens, and thereby fulfill the law of Christ. For if anyone thinks he is something when he is nothing, he deceives himself. But each one must examine his own work, and then he will have reason for boasting in regard to himself alone, and not in regard to another. (Galatians 6:1–4 NASB)

For if you forgive others for their transgressions, your heavenly Father will also forgive you. But if you do not forgive others, then your Father will not forgive your transgressions. (Matthew 6:14–15 NASB)

God's Antivirus Program
Grace and Mercy

God is love. Let me say that again: God is love! Stop and think about that. No, I mean really stop. Stop and think about that! Spend some time meditating on these verses.

But God demonstrates His own love toward us, in that while we were yet sinners, Christ died for us. Much more then, having now been justified by His blood, we shall be saved from the wrath of God through Him. For if while we were enemies we were reconciled to God through the death of His Son, much more, having been reconciled, we shall be saved by His life. And not only this, but we also exult in God through our Lord Jesus Christ, through whom we have now received the reconciliation. (Romans 5:8–11 NASB)

See how great a love the Father has bestowed on us, that we would be called children of God; and such we are. For this reason the world does not know us, because it did not know Him.(1 John 3:1 NASB)

It is this great love that causes God to relate to us on the basis of grace and mercy. It is this great love that gives us the ability to show grace and mercy to others. (Read again in the chapter on spiritual values about "We are designed to be part of His body, the church.")

Grace and mercy are the antiviruses that destroy the viruses of guilt and condemnation. Grace can be defined as giving someone a good thing that he or she does not deserve. Mercy can be defined as not giving someone a bad thing that he or she does deserve. When we live in the love and grace and mercy of God, we will live in freedom finding favor with God and man.

Listen Up, Satan!

Next time you start feeling satanic guilt and shame, read these verses out loud to Satan. He will not stick around to listen.

But He gives a greater grace. Therefore it says, "God is opposed to the proud, but gives grace to the humble." Submit therefore to God. Resist the devil and he will flee from you. Draw near to God and He will draw near to you. Cleanse your hands, you sinners; and purify your hearts, you double-minded. (James 4:6–8 NASB)

But where sin increased, grace abounded all the more, so that, as sin reigned in death, even so grace would reign through righteousness to eternal life through Jesus Christ our Lord. (Romans 5:20–21 NASB)

Therefore let us draw near with confidence to the throne of grace, so that we may receive mercy and find grace to help in time of need. (Hebrews 4:16 NASB)

May grace and peace be yours in the fullest measure.

Blessed be the God and Father of our Lord Jesus Christ, who according to His great mercy has caused us to be born again to a living hope through the resurrection of Jesus Christ from the dead. (1 Peter 1:2–3 NASB)

He saved us, not on the basis of deeds which we have done in righteousness, but according to His mercy, by the washing of regeneration and renewing by the Holy Spirit, whom He poured out upon us richly through Jesus Christ our Savior, so that being justified by His grace we would be made heirs according to the hope of eternal life. (Titus 3:5–7 NASB)

Practice Makes Perfect

There is no shortcut to maturity. It takes practice. The Greek word *teleios*, often translated "perfect," means to be complete or mature. Maturity comes from practice.

We don't realize it, but practice is actually planned failure. Think about it. If we did not know we were going to fail, then why would we need to practice? Each failure brings us a little closer to perfection/maturity. Practice develops physical and mental muscle memory. The more we practice right thinking and right behavior, the more it becomes automatic. If we do not fail, we will never succeed.

Michael Jordan-Success through Failure
www.livingthatmattersbook.com/37.html

How?

It is my prayer that you will commit your life to practicing living in God's design. You will fail. I pray that you will do so in freedom, without fear of failure. I pray that you will learn to think generationally, working to influence your children and grandchildren first and then the body of Christ and then the entire world to live by God's design.

"Only give heed to yourself and keep your soul diligently, so that you do not forget the things which your eyes have seen and they do not depart from your heart all the days of your life; but make them known to your sons and your grandsons." (Deuteronomy 4:9 NASB)

"Now this is the commandment, the statutes and the judgments which the LORD your God has commanded me to teach you, that you might do them in the land where you are going over to possess it, so that you and your son and your grandson might fear the Lord your God, to keep all His statutes and His commandments which I command you, all the days of your life, and that your days may be prolonged. (Deuteronomy 6: 1–2 NASB)

Did you notice at the end of every chapter, I have said, **"To be continued"**? Each chapter is to be continued by you. Spend the rest of your life adding to each value your unique experiences and illustrations and biblical truths, along with family history. Then pass it on to your children, so they will add to it and pass it on to their children. ... *To be continued*!!!!!!

**And last of all, never forget,
it's not about:**

Me,	**(Spiritual Values)**
Us,	**(Relational Values)**
Them,	**(Parental Values)**
My Body,	**(Sexual Values)**
Money,	**(Financial Values)**

It is all about God!!!!!

**If that is not true ... then please
throw this book in the trash!**

15 VALUES
(It's not about me; it's about God)

Top Three Spiritual Values

1. *We are designed for intimate fellowship with God.*

2. *We are designed to be part of His body, the church.*

3. *We are designed to love the world in His name.*

Top Three Relational Values

1. *It's not about us. It's about God.*

2. *The roles of husband, as played by man, and wife, as played by woman, reflect God through authority and submission.*

3. *God sees you as one. Divorce is not part of His design.*

Top Three Parental Values

1. *It's not about us; it's about them.*
   It's not about them; it's about God.

2. *A mother and a father is a parent.*

3. *Godly parenting is about discipline, resulting in godliness, not about punishment, controlling behavior.*

The Top Three Sexual Values

1. *My body does not belong to me; it belongs to God. It will either reflect or dishonor His glory.*

2. *Through sexuality a husband and wife reflect the glory and image of God to each other.*

3. *The male body and the female body are designed to become one flesh. They fit together to reflect the glory and image of God through creation.*

The Top Three Financial Values

1. *Everything belongs to God; nothing belongs to me. I am a steward of His assets.*

2. *The world operates on a system of buying and selling. God operates on a system of giving and receiving.*

3. *Living in the body of Christ is true communism.*

The Only
Living That Matters
Is
Living by God's Design

CPSIA information can be obtained
at www.ICGtesting.com
Printed in the USA
FSOW01n1433211015
12434FS